Against All Odds

Against All Odds

The Struggle for Racial Integration in Religious Organizations

Brad Christerson, Korie L. Edwards, and Michael O. Emerson

NEW YORK UNIVERSITY PRESS
New York and London

NEW YORK UNIVERSITY PRESS
New York and London

Library of Congress Cataloging-in-Publication Data
Christerson, Brad.
Against all odds : the struggle for racial integration in
religious organizations / Brad Christerson, Korie L. Edwards, and
Michael O. Emerson.
p. cm.
Includes bibliographical references and index.
ISBN 0–8147–2223–7 (hardcover : alk. paper) —
ISBN 0–8147–2224–5 (pbk. : alk. paper)
1. Race relations—Religious aspects—Christianity—Case studies.
2. Religious institutions—United States—Case studies.
3. United States—Race relations—Case studies.   I. Edwards, Korie
L.   II. Emerson, Michael O., 1965–   III. Title.
BR517.C46   2004
277.3'083'089—dc22   2004017786

New York University Press books are printed on acid-free paper,
and their binding materials are chosen for strength and durability.

Manufactured in the United States of America
c 10 9 8 7 6 5 4 3 2 1
p 10 9 8 7 6 5 4 3 2 1

To Norma Christerson,
an inspiration to all of us

Contents

Acknowledgments ix

1   Against All Odds 1

2   The Need for Belonging 9

3   A Place to Call Home 36

4   White Flight or Flux? 58

5   Embrace and Division 80

6   Together and Separate 104

7   Jesus Is Color-Blind 126

8   What We Learned 151

Notes 187

References 189

Index 193

About the Authors 197

Acknowledgments

This volume has been a collaborative work in every sense; all authors have contributed equally. Many other people have contributed as well. We would like to thank the organizations and the many people who allowed us to enter their lives in our efforts to learn about their experiences. We owe them a debt of gratitude for their time and honest sharing. We are grateful to the head persons of these organizations for opening their doors to enable this study to occur. Thanks also to our research assistants on this project, especially Sasha Woo, Jessica Lundgren, and Dan Dehanas, who did wonderful work. The project would have been difficult to complete without their expert help. Special thanks to Carley and Danae Christerson, who "helped Dad study churches" by visiting the children's programs in our cases, and to Carin Christerson for her editorial comments.

We wish to express our thanks to our editor, Jennifer Hammer. She was wonderful to work with, and helped guide us through the process of writing this book. We appreciate her efforts to secure an early contract on the promise of this manuscript, which enormously benefited the process of writing and gave us a clear goal. Finally, we would like to thank the Louisville Institute, whose generous funding made this book possible.

During the final writing of this book, we learned that Brad Christerson's mother was very ill with cancer. This difficult news reminded us all in a powerful way of the importance of family. To all of our families, we love and appreciate you. You are precious.

1

Against All Odds

The leaders of a small multiracial congregation in Los Angeles County have called a special meeting on Sunday afternoon. The purpose of the meeting is to have an open dialogue among members about how the racial and ethnic diversity of the church affects the congregation.

A Filipina woman begins by stating that she feels the church, while diverse in membership, is not diverse in the sense that all of the cultures in the congregation are equally valued and represented in the way God is worshipped. An African American woman agrees, saying that she feels constrained by the worship style—she cannot express her love for God in the expressive style she is used to. Filipino and white members respond to her by saying—"we want you to worship however you want; if you want to dance and shout Amen, please do." She is frustrated by this response, as they seem to have missed her point—that the environment of worship at this church is not conducive to expressive worship.

These two women, as they share their experiences in the church, touch off an avalanche of heartfelt sharing about the difficulties and struggles different members of the congregation have been experiencing but have not felt comfortable expressing. This dialogue about racial dynamics is the first such discussion this interracial church had had in its three-year existence.

A number of white members are annoyed by the lack of attention paid to punctuality and organization in the way the church has been run. An African American member laments the lack of interest in the congregation toward serving and engaging the surrounding community. A number of people complain that members of the largest ethnic group, Filipinos, are exclusive and "cliquey" in their friendships.

Emotions are running high and hurts are being revealed and discussed openly. One member describes this gathering as the most intense he has ever attended. After the meeting, some members question whether the church should be focusing on these emotional issues that could divide them. Others express relief at having finally been able to express the pent-up frustrations that have been building up for so long, and at the fact that a dialogue about the difficulties in racially integrating a religious organization seems finally to be happening. The leaders of this small congregation are realizing for the first time, with piercing clarity, what they have gotten themselves into by trying to establish an interracial religious organization.

This book is an attempt to probe the sensitive nerve that was touched at this Sunday afternoon church meeting in Los Angeles. It is a vexing issue both nationally and worldwide. How can organizations incorporate separate racial, ethnic, and culture groups? Should they? What is the experience for people and groups in such organizations? Many people, and many organizations, grapple with such questions. Whether it is the integration of public schools, major corporations, or country clubs, issues around race and inclusivity have occupied a major position in U.S. society, and in a number of societies around the world, for decades. Debates swirl around such often loosely defined and easily misunderstood terms as separation, desegregation, pluralism, integration, and assimilation. Which of these processes lead to greater equality among groups, or does greater equality lead to some of these processes? What are the costs and benefits of these processes for the individuals and groups involved in them, and for society as a whole? Throughout the history of the United States, people have died, have been killed, defending or working for one or more of these processes. They are serious business.

The purpose of this book is to address some of the key questions and issues faced by modern diverse nations by taking a close, careful look at one type of organization—religious organizations. Our aim is to provide rich firsthand accounts of the sociological forces that make racially integrated organizations difficult to sustain, and of the beliefs, practices, and structures that allow these organizations to survive and thrive despite their difficulties. We will hear, through the voices of the people in these organizations, the joys and frustrations arising from actually attempting to live racial integration. We will ask how they came to be in such organizations, and why they stay (or leave). Based on analyses of these voices in multiple contexts, we develop a theoretical framework for understanding the dynamics of major processes in interracial religious organizations. In short, we aim to provide readers of this book with an inside, visceral sense of what it is like to be part of a multiracial religious organization and a theoretical understanding of these experiences and organizations.

Why Study Religious Organizations?

In the United States, religious organizations are ubiquitous. With more than 350,000 congregations of many faith traditions, thousands of religious schools from preschool to graduate school, and thousands of other para-congregational organizations, religious organizations involve millions and millions of Americans. They also occupy vital roles in American ethnic and immigration life, often serving as key locations for adaptation to the United States (Ebaugh and Chavez 2000).

What is more, religious organizations occupy a unique place in U.S. civil society, serving as vital mediating forces between the small, private worlds of individual and family and the mass, public worlds of government, the economy, and public education. Much has been written on the important roles mediating organizations play in bridging the disparate spheres of the public and the private, in allowing democracy to function (e.g., Wuthnow and Evans 2002), in generating and organizing volunteer labor and other social capital (Cnaan 2002; Putnam 2000), and in serving as key locations for identity formation, meaning, and social networks (Emerson forthcoming; Olson 1993).

Religious organizations, as the nation's largest volunteer organizations, are essential players in U.S. race relations, both contemporarily and historically (Emerson and Smith 2000). Moreover, their volunteer nature allows us to study what people do when given the opportunity to choose their affiliations and participation levels. This characteristic stands in stark contrast to most institutions and organizations, such as mandatory primary and secondary schooling, competitively selective higher education and work, and price-exclusionary housing markets. In non-volunteer organizations, the patterns and processes of racial and ethnic relations and representation are impacted in various ways by these other factors. But religious organizations, because they are voluntary and because they involve more than half of all Americans, provide us with perhaps our clearest opportunity for studying the processes of segregation, desegregation, integration, assimilation, and pluralism in American organizational ʃing such organizations allows us to see what people do when ᴄᴄy are free to choose with whom to associate.

Because of the wide range of choices (Finke and Stark 1992), and the freedom to make those choices, it is perhaps not surprising that religious organizations are the most segregated institutions in U.S. life (Emerson forthcoming). For example, about 90 percent of congregations are at least 90 percent one race (Emerson and Smith 2000). For this reason, to study the process of integration in religious organizations is to examine a rare event, to study something that exists against all odds. Focusing on religious organizations allows us to see what forces are necessary, apart from law or coercion, for organizations to be racially and ethnically integrated. To study these organizations, then, has the potential to teach us *something new about racial and ethnic relations,* something we could not learn by focusing on neighborhoods, schools, government, the military, or places of employment.

How Can We Go About Such a Study?

We had many choices about how to approach our study. Because we knew little about the process of integration and racial and ethnic diversity in congregations (see Ammerman 1997; Becker 1999; Dougherty 2003 for exceptions) and have little theory to guide us, we used what is called the case study method. We selected four congregations, a university-based religious organization, and a religiously-based university. We studied the history of these six organizations, attempted to understand how they became racially and ethnically diverse, and, through interviews, focused on people's experiences in these organizations. Specifically, our case studies were oriented around the following questions:

What are the reasons people give for choosing to be involved in multiracial religious organizations as opposed to homogeneous organizations?

What are the added benefits, both spiritual and social, that accrue to members of multiracial religious organizations as a result of their involvement?

What are the costs and difficulties involved in maintaining a healthy and functioning multiracial religious organization? Which groups within the organizations tend to pay the highest costs of maintenance?

What, if any, are the specific practices that appear to make the maintenance of a healthy and functioning multiracial religious organization
more likely?

Each substantive chapter to follow focuses on one religious organization's
experiences of and answers to these questions. We use our case studies to
help us identify commonalities and differences across these organizations.
In the concluding chapter, we not only reflect on the commonalities and
differences, but begin working toward a theory of integration—specifically in religious organizations, but also more generally, in organizations
of all types. The case study method makes our concluding chapter possible; in turn, this concluding chapter will allow for further and more complete testing and research in the future. The case study method also makes
for interesting reading, as the individual cases afford an inside look at
these organizations and their people. Readers undoubtedly will learn
from the case studies in ways not anticipated or touched on in the discussions we present.

Selecting the Cases

Though on the surface selecting the cases seems mundane, much of this
book's value rests on the careful selection of appropriate cases to study.
We had several factors to consider. We needed to balance having a diversity of cases with our need for enough commonalities in them that we
could separate racial from other processes. Six cases studies seemed the
proper number: enough cases to see variation, but not too many to over-
whelm the value of in-depth case studies. We wanted regional variation,
but again we did not want six different localities (which we felt would in-
troduce yet another variable—we would not know if differences were a
result of the organizational practices and people in that organization, or
more generally of the region in which the organization was located). We
settled on what we call a *decreasing stack* method. We chose three cases
in southern California, two in the Houston area, and one in a large mid-
western metropolitan area. We chose to locate all of our cases in large
metropolitan areas because this is currently where the overwhelming majority of racially diverse religious organizations are located. We suspect
this large metropolitan dominance will decline over time, as the racial and
ethnic diversity of the United States is reflected more and more in subur-

ban and rural communities as well as cities. For now, however, our cases are all in highly diverse large metropolitan areas.

Our next decision was what should be the ratio of congregations to non-congregations in our sample. Because congregations account for the majority of religious organizations, we wanted the majority of our cases to be congregations. However, we needed more than one non-congregation religious organization represented in our sample. So we settled on four congregations and two other religious organizations. These two other cases provide an important point of comparison, an opportunity to consider whether the processes identified in the congregations are the same or are modified in a non-congregation religious setting.

Perhaps our most important decision was what religious tradition(s) our cases should come from. The United States is a highly religiously diverse nation in terms of the variety of groups and traditions (Eck 2001), but most of this diversity in terms of numbers is found in different forms of the same tradition—Christianity (Beaman 2003). About 90 percent of religious people in the United States claim a Christian affiliation, with no other religion having more than a 3 percent share (Emerson and Kim 2003). Weighing our goals for this book, our number of cases, and the variations we have already discussed, we decided we had to locate our cases within one faith tradition. To do otherwise would have introduced far too many complexities into the interpretation of our findings.

Perhaps in part because it is so dominant, Christianity in the United States falls into several largely separate traditions. Catholic, mainline Protestant, and evangelical Protestant are the main categories; some analysts also include separate categories such as black Protestant and Pentecostal Protestant. To reduce the nubmer of variables between cases, we needed to locate all of our case studies within one of these traditions. We chose the evangelical Protestant tradition for two reasons. First, in terms of organizations and people, it is currently largest of these Christian traditions.[1] Second, because one of us (Emerson) had previously studied evangelicals and race (Emerson and Smith 2000), locating our case studies within this tradition gave us the richest theoretical base and point of departure.

We recognize that in studying just one faith tradition we jeopardize our ability to generalize beyond that tradition. We reflect on the broader applicability of our findings in the concluding chapter.

Within the guidelines of the factors discussed above, we selected our

TABLE 1.1
Case Summary

	Organizational Type	Metro	Size	Racial Composition	Current Type	Founding Type
Messiah	Congregation	Los Angeles	150	55% Asian 30% Anglo 10% Latino 5% Other	Asian majority	Asian
Crosstown	Congregation	Midwest city**	220	65% Black 30% Anglo 5% Other	Black majority	Anglo
Wilcrest	Congregation	Houston	500	42% Anglo 30% Latino 20% Black 5% Asian 3% Other	Anglo plurality	Anglo
Brookside	Congregation	Los Angeles	300	55% Latino 30% Anglo 15% Black	Latino majority	Anglo
Emmanuel Bible College	College	Southern California	3,000	75% Anglo 10% Latino 10% Asian 5% Black	Anglo majority	Anglo
Christ in Action	Campus student group*	Houston	50	45% Asian 45% Anglo 10% Other	No majority	Anglo

NOTE: Names of, and minor facts about, the organizations were changed to protect anonymity.
*Religious group on non-sectarian campus
** Name of city withheld to protect anonymity of organization.

cases to vary in racial and ethnic composition, and in size of organization, as these factors may influence the process and experience of integration. Subsequent chapters afford in-depth looks at each of the cases, but by way of introduction Table 1.1 presents a summary of the six organizations studied.

Summary

Our aim in this book is to understand the processes that occur when members of different racial groups come together within organizations.

Our focus is on volunteer religious organizations. These organizations afford us a unique opportunity to study the processes of desegregation and integration and to better understand race relations. We begin by traveling to suburban Los Angeles, into the world of Messiah Fellowship, the congregation in which the intense meeting that began this chapter took place. What factors led up to that meeting? Let us find out.

2

The Need for Belonging

Forty or so members of Messiah Fellowship are packed into a suburban home in Los Angeles County, milling around, laughing, and joking. A group of eight young men are scattered around the floor in front of the TV watching the end of a basketball game, periodically yelling in happiness or disgust at the events unfolding on the screen. Folks mingle together as large packs of young children run in and out of the sliding glass door to the back yard. Young boys chase each other with plastic swords while the girls take turns climbing up the ladder to the slide attached to the swing set. Groups of young women stand together and swap stories about their week. People weave their way through the crowd to the food table in the kitchen where a large pan of chicken, flour tortillas, and salsa from a local Mexican restaurant are available as a make-your-own-burrito buffet line. A giant birthday cake on a separate table—for the pastor's son, age 5—signals the reason for this celebration. The room is loud, crowded, playful, and full of laughter. An outsider would immediately see that this is a crowd of people who enjoy one another.

The room is also surprisingly racially mixed. About half are Filipino, including the hosts of the party, and the rest are a mix of whites, Latinos, Koreans, Africans, and African Americans. A racially mixed birthday party is not that uncommon in Los Angeles County—its inner-ring suburbs are some of the most diverse cities in the nation. What is remarkable about this party is the appearance that this is a large interracial extended family gathering together to celebrate the birthday of one of their own. It is a picture proponents of racial integration would like very much—people from the same city, from different races, all together in a home, sharing their lives together.

Birthday parties play an important role for most Filipino families. It is a chance to get all of the extended family, friends, and acquaintances together for a long Saturday of food, games, catching up on each other's lives, and laughing together for hours. Unlike birthday parties for white

American kids—which tend to be short, small gatherings of the child's closest friends and their moms, oriented around structured activities for the kids—Filipino birthday parties are as much for the family and friends as for the kids. They are large, informal, unstructured, and last from early afternoon well into the night. They also provide consistently occurring occasions for friends to be with each other and to socialize. For members of Messiah Fellowship, these frequent parties provide opportunities to get to know and bond with their fellow church members. What is puzzling about this church, however, is that despite the high turnout and warm atmosphere at these frequent gatherings, it continues to lose members to other churches because those members feel socially isolated.

A New Kind of Church

Messiah Fellowship is a young interracial middle-class congregation, most of whose members grew up in L.A. County in the 1970s and 1980s—a time of profound racial transformation. Los Angeles County went from being 80 percent white in 1960 to 38 percent white in 1990 to 31 percent white in 2000. Hispanics are now the largest ethnic group in the county, and there are thirty-four different ethnic groups that have numbers of five thousand or more in the county. Many of Messiah's members, therefore, have grown up in racially diverse schools and now work in racially diverse environments. The racial mix at this party is nothing new to these people. What is new to them is the sharing and living out their spiritual lives in a racially diverse congregation. Despite growing up in diverse schools, most have only had contact with racially homogeneous churches. As is true in the rest of America, L.A.'s churches are highly segregated by race and ethnicity.

Messiah grew out of a network of friends who wanted to start something different, a "new kind of church." The founding pastor of the church, Eddie Ramos, was born in the Philippines but moved to the Echo Park neighborhood of Los Angeles in the 1970s when he was in elementary school. Eddie's father, like many other Filipino men during that period, was able to gain a work visa to the United States because of his training as an engineer. As the family prospered, they moved from Echo Park to a racially diverse middle-class suburb in south L.A. County. Eddie grew up Catholic, like most Filipinos, but he and his older brother both had a conversion experience through an evangelical campus ministry at the local junior college they were attending. Eddie then transferred to a local California State University campus and became a leader in the same evangelical ministry group at that campus, which at the time consisted mostly of Asian and white students. Following graduation, he became a youth minister at a medium-sized Filipino church in suburban L.A. County, and he served in that position while pursuing a graduate degree at a local evangelical seminary.

Eddie's experience as the youth minister at the Filipino church began to put seeds in his mind of starting something different. The church where he worked consisted mostly of first- and 1.5- (born overseas but lived in America since childhood) generation immigrants. There is a feel of tradition and protocol at his old church; the younger members look up to and respect the older members, while the older members feel a sense of responsibility to care for and lead the younger members. The pastor is the direct source of most of the activities at this church; he does everything from preaching on Sunday, to leading most of the fellowship groups, to doing almost all of the church administrative duties, to caring for individual members. Socially, the older members are expected to lead and set examples for the young, and the young are expected to respect and be led by the older members, particularly those in church leadership. Tagalog is often mixed with English in conversations, and sometimes from the pulpit.

Eddie and a number of his friends from college, as well as other members of his church, envisioned a more racially and culturally mixed church. They also wanted a less hierarchical congregation, where all church members were both free to and expected to contribute and lead corporate worship and ministry groups, rather than having most things led by the appointed pastor and elders.

Eddie began meeting with an informal group of around fifteen friends and family members to explore the idea of starting a new church. Around half of this group was from the Filipino church where Eddie worked; the other half were Eddie's friends from the evangelical ministry groups at the junior college and the state university. These founding members decided they wanted a church that would be welcoming to all people, a place where all different types of people would feel comfortable. Most of them had friends of different ethnicities and wanted a place where these friends would feel welcome if they invited them to church. A number of these original group members were also in mixed-race marriages and had tried different churches but had felt uncomfortable in monoethnic congregations. In one such couple, for example, the husband (white) did not feel comfortable in the Filipino churches they tried and the wife (Filipino) felt uncomfortable in the white churches they visited. Many of these people, then, felt most comfortable in mixed environments. Most members of the original group were under thirty.

There was no organized plan put forward, however, to attract an interracial following. Since the people in this diverse group were all friends and were involved in various churches and ministries together, it seemed natural to them that if they were welcoming to all people, the church would end up being multiethnic.

In addition to intending the church to be welcoming to all people, core group members wanted a church that was less hierarchical and rigid in its structure, allowing for participation by all members. Finally, and most importantly to the leaders, they desired a church that was really committed to reaching out to non-Christians and telling them the good news about Jesus.

This group of friends met informally for about a year, after which Messiah Fellowship was officially born. The church met in the clubhouse of a park for the first few months, then moved to an elementary school. At the end of the first year, average worship attendance was in the fifty to sixty range. Most of the regular attenders were young (early to late twenties) and had come to the church after hearing about it from friends who were attending.

Messiah also grew in racial diversity. Through the diverse friendship networks of the original members, the church recruited a number of Latinos, Anglos, Chinese, and African Americans. The church also attracted a racially diverse group of students from a local evangelical college who were looking for a multiethnic church close to their school. During this first year, the church was overflowing with youthful energy and an optimistic sense of possibility—that this could be a new kind of church, one that was a reflection of what heaven would be like and that would unleash the gifts and talents of each of its diverse members for the greater benefit of all.

A Taste of Heaven

As the years began to pass, the church continued to grow in numbers and in diversity. Average worship attendance now is about 120, about half of whom are Filipino, around 30 percent are white, and the rest are a mix of Latino, African American, African, and other Asian. The church is also young—almost all of the members are under forty, and the majority are under thirty.

While there had never been an intentional plan for the church to become interracial (other than a commitment to being welcoming to everyone), racial diversity became central to its identity. All but a few of the members we interviewed stated either that diversity was the main reason they started coming to the church or that it was the thing they enjoyed most about it. Many of these congregants also reported a profound sense of spiritual enrichment from worshiping in a diverse environment. One Latino member said:

> It's a taste of heaven on earth to have people from all these different backgrounds worshipping together. I feel like my worship of God is so much more pure and authentic when I look up there and see all of the nations represented.

Other members concurred:

> It's awesome. You get to interact with people from other cultures. We get to know their culture, at least in a small way. It proves how awesome God is that He can bring us all together. (Filipino)

> I appreciate that it's a multi-ethnic church. I've never seen a church like that before. It's like church is supposed to be—the body of Christ all together. All of the other churches I've been to are one ethnic group. (Filipino)

Another member perceived theological significance in the diversity of the congregation:

> It's truer to the biblical model in I Corinthians with the body of Christ. We need each other. And it's an example to the world. You know people in the neighborhood see us walking from our cars to our church and can see that people can be together. It's a statement to the world. (White)

Others stated that they could no longer imagine themselves in a homogeneous congregation:

I don't feel comfortable in an all-white church. I don't know why. Maybe it's because I haven't been in a while. It's boring to me. (White)

Churches with just one ethnicity don't get it. They're complacent with where they are and people are happy with the way things are done. But it's not like it's going to be in heaven. (African American)

It's theologically more authentic to have a multi-ethnic church in a place like L.A. It's counterintuitive, I guess, to have a homogeneous church in a diverse environment. I feel like it is a better witness to the secular society, and I find comfort in inviting people from different backgrounds. (White)

Clearly, these members are enriched spiritually by attending this congregation.

But after five years of existence, some of the youthful energy and optimism has faded and some of the original members have left the church. Nevertheless, the hopes of Eddie and the founding members are still alive as the church struggles onward toward their goal of a welcoming, non-hierarchical, and evangelistic congregation. The church, however, has struggled in recent years with a number of obstacles to the fulfillment of its goals, many of which we believe have arisen from the racial diversity of the church.

A Lack of Connection

One of the central goals of Eddie and the founders was that this congregation would be friendly and embracing of whoever came to the church. They did not have a structured plan to make this happen—leaders simply encouraged that the regular members make an effort to greet new people, remember their names, and try to include them in whatever might be going on at the church.

Most churches would say that this is a high priority for them—to welcome anyone into their midst, and to love and embrace them as is commanded in the Bible. Most churches would also say that anyone, of any ethnic group, is welcome and that all groups should be treated with the same love and affirmation. Yet, most churches remain ethnically and racially homogeneous. Messiah became diverse through the diverse friendship networks of the founding pastor, and it grew more diverse as more and more people became excited about the prospect of being involved in an interracial congregation. Yet despite the efforts of the church to be warm and embracing, the biggest obstacle in its five-year history seems to have been that many of its members feel socially isolated at the church. This has caused many of them to leave the congregation.

While a few of the Filipinos we interviewed mentioned that they did not feel like they had many close friendships in the church, the sense of isolation was clearly more acute among non-Filipinos. Of the seventeen non-Filipinos we interviewed, fourteen spoke of struggles and frustrations relating to others in the church and of not feeling connected socially. In contrast, only two of the nine Filipinos we interviewed mentioned having difficulty interacting with others, and neither of those two felt a lack of close ties in the church. Three of the four people we interviewed who had left the church (all non-Filipino) cited lack of friendships as their primary reason for leaving.

The majority of the non-Filipinos we interviewed spoke very openly of their discouragement in trying to fit in socially at the church. In particular, they said that the core of the church is made up of Filipinos who seem to have strong family and friendship groups, and that they feel shut out of those groups.

> For a long time I didn't have friends at church. I felt really out of place. I tried to understand the Filipino mentality and relate, but I couldn't do it. I was trying to fit in. I even started to try to dress sort of like them and act like them, but I couldn't fit in. (White)

> I have at different times been disillusioned by the difficulty fitting in. I'm an extrovert and get to know people easily, but I feel shut out. I still feel that certain groups are impenetrable. (African immigrant)

> [The church] seems kind of friendly at first. People come and talk to you and try to remember your name. But when you decide to become a part of the church, you have to do all the work to get into the in-group. . . . I'm an outgoing person and I'm really adaptable. I get to know people pretty easily. But [this church] is a totally different story. It's like you hit this wall. I have to totally extend myself to get to know people. (African American)

There isn't a sense of family or community there. It shouldn't have taken me this long to feel like I know people. I've been going for two years and just now I feel like I have friends at church. People say hi to you and are friendly, but there isn't enough interaction. It's not a family. (Hispanic)

The Filipino relationship structure and ethic makes it hard for people outside of that to break in. . . . The founders of the church have a really tight group. (African immigrant)

The Filipinos seem real group oriented. It seems hard to get involved in their groups. They have strong family ties and a lot of them are related, while other people kind of straggle in and so it's hard for them to get into those strong groups. They feel comfortable with each other, but I feel like an outsider to those groups. (White)

Other non-Filipino members expressed worry that their kids were not fitting in with their Filipino peers. Although the church is only half Filipino, a substantial majority of the children in the church are Filipino.

Another thing is [our daughter] doesn't have friends at church. Kids won't play with her and she says the kids don't like her. I think a lot of it is that a lot of the Filipino kids are cousins and they see each other all the time. So it's hard to break in to that. (White)

The Filipino families—many of them are related or close friends—and so they see each other all the time. Their kids all play together and it doesn't seem like they really pay much attention to any other kids. Some of those kids have told [our daughter] that she can't play with them. (White)

Of the five people we interviewed who had left the church, four cited this "lack of connection" as their reason for leaving. Interestingly, all four are currently attending or looking for another interracial church.

This lack of relational connection that so many non-Filipino members expressed is not easily visible from the surface. Based on a visit to a birthday party like the one we described at the beginning of the chapter, it would appear that these are people who enjoy one another's company and are deeply committed to each other. Yet the majority of non-Filipinos seem to be experiencing this lack of belonging. In contrast, most of the Filipino members we interviewed expressed that the relationships they have with people at church is one of the most enjoyable aspects of their involvement at Messiah. When a Filipino female was asked what she enjoyed about being at the church, she responded, "Friendships. We can be around people and tell them what's going on in our lives and they won't gossip, but they'll just try to help you." And a Filipino male said, "I enjoy the relationships I have with people on the worship team. I have great fellowship with them." Another Filipino male said, "I love the family aspect. . . . I like the fellowship after church—fellowship is key for me at this church."

The consensus among the non-Filipino members we interviewed is that the Filipinos at church, particularly those who are in leadership and are part of the original founding group, have tight friendship networks within the church from which non-Filipinos are excluded. This conclusion is supported by other data we collected at this church. We asked thirty-eight members to name their three closest friends within the church and their three closest friends outside of the church, in rank order. We then asked them whether their number one friend inside the church was closer to them than their number one friend outside the church; we repeated the questions for their number two and number three friends. The results reveal that Filipinos are much more likely to have their closest friends inside of the church, while non-Filipinos are much more likely to have their closest friends outside of the church (table 2.1). In addition, Filipino church members are much more likely to be best friends with other Filipinos, while non-Filipinos are more likely to have cross-race friendships within the church (table 2.2). This finding supports the notion that it is difficult to break into Filipino friendship networks within the church.

Differences in Social Interaction

If there are Filipino friendship groups that exclude non-Filipinos at this church, it is certainly not a conscious or intentional desire on the part of the Filipinos. The Filipino members who are seen as hard to get to know expressed repeatedly to us how important it is for all to love each other and to be "one in Christ." They also maintained that they love the fact that the church allows them to get to know people of different backgrounds. One of these members told us:

TABLE 2.1
Comparison of Strength of Respondents' Friendships
Inside and Outside of Church

	Non-Filipino Members	Filipino Members
% who chose #1 friend within church as being closer than #1 friend outside	32	58*
% who chose #2 friend within church as being closer than #2 friend outside	37	68**
% who chose #3 friend within church as being closer than #3 friend outside	47	53

NOTES: Pearson's Chi-Square test. Difference between Filipino and non-Filipino members significant at (* p < .1, ** p < .05, *** p < .01).

TABLE 2.2
Ethnicity of Respondents' Best Friends within Church (n = 38)

	Non-Filipino Members	Filipino Members
% whose #1 friend within church is same ethnicity as respondent	53	84**
% whose #2 friend within church is same ethnicity as respondent	42	79**
% whose #3 friend within church is same ethnicity as respondent	32	84***

NOTES: Pearson's Chi-Square test. Difference between Filipino and non-Filipino members significant at (* p < .1, ** p < .05, *** p < .01).

Filipino member: I enjoy it. Everyone can see past skin color. It's not like Filipino churches where everyone's speaking the language, and if you don't speak it you feel out of it. We can learn from different people and can learn about different cultures.

Interviewer: So it doesn't make anything more difficult?

Filipino member: I don't think so. It makes everyone realize we have the same purpose, even though we've all been brought up differently.

Yet despite the enjoyment of getting to know people from different cultures and the sincere desire to be unified, the divide remains.

We probed the non-Filipinos who felt a lack of connection, asking why they felt that way and what they thought the reasons were for this relational isolation. Their responses did not indicate that they felt that the Filipinos were intentionally excluding them out of racial or any other motivation. Most cited differences in ways of interacting, and a different way of viewing friendship.

One comment that recurred frequently was that the Filipinos seem to have "superficial" friendships. One Filipino male who was in a mixed-race marriage expressed the difference he sees between Filipino friendships and those of other ethnicities:

> We [Filipinos] seem friendly on the outside. But it's a hollow friendliness. It's all activities and fun stuff. There is no depth to relationships. We're very friendly. We're activity driven. Our spiritual life is defined by what we're doing rather than deep personal relationships. We have fun. We have a big need for events and parties all the time.

This statement, that Filipinos are very friendly and love to have fun but are hard to know on more than a "surface" level was echoed repeatedly among the non-Filipinos.

> But then there's the 30-something Filipino crowd with families and kids, and I just can't relate. I can't carry on a conversation with them. Maybe they see friendship differently than we do. I don't know if they share very deeply with each other. But I feel like I hit this wall that I can't get through. (White)

> It's hard to connect on a deep level when you're in a larger group setting, doing something social. It's kind of a downer when someone shares deeply, maybe about something they're going through, when you're in a "fun" environment. It gets awkward. (White)

> It is really difficult for me to connect with Filipino women. We had a "date night" with [a Bible study group consisting mostly of Filipino married couples]. We had a really good time, we played games, we laughed, we had fun. But it was like pulling teeth trying to have a conversation. It's hard to get to know Filipinos deeply. It's like pulling teeth. It's uncomfortable. At Messiah I felt like I didn't fit in. I was lonely. (Chinese-American)

It appears that many of the non-Filipino church members were seeking more one-on-one, "therapeutic" relationships where a fairly deep level of vulnerable sharing takes place quickly, and they felt that the Filipino members were less open to that type of relationship.

> It was a new experience for me being around Filipinos. Filipinos are more—if you have a problem you don't show it. Everyone seems to always be doing well. It's hard to know when people aren't doing well. Whereas white people more wear their hearts on their sleeves. So there is an issue of openness there. (White)

Another obstacle to social connection at the church between Filipinos and non-Filipinos seems to be the tradition of hierarchical social relationships. Non-Filipinos referred to it as the *"kuya ate* thing." Traditional Filipino social relationships are analogous to family relationships, where an older friend is called *kuya* or *ate* (big brother or big sister) and is therefore to be looked up to and respected and sought out for advice, while younger members are to be looked after and cared for. This pattern is an extension of the roles played within nuclear families. Often the oldest child must be respected and obeyed by the younger children within the family, and the eldest is responsible for caring for their younger siblings. A number of the respondents interviewed felt that this tradition creates certain barriers to close friendships between church members of different ages.

> Interviewer: You mentioned the Filipino relationship structure and ethic—could you explain what you mean by that?
>
> African immigrant member: Yes, the whole kuya and ate tradition. I can relate to it, because in Africa if someone is older than you, they are like your uncle or aunt, but it creates a distance and protocol to the relationship. If I need support from an older person, I wouldn't know if I could share anything too deep with them.

One respondent was particularly frustrated with this aspect of social interaction at the church:

> And the ate and kuya thing drives me nuts. I think the whole concept is ridiculous. That if you have a sister that is one year older than you, you have to be respectful and submissive to them. Since I'm older, everyone sees me as a mom. It makes it hard to have friends. (White)

A white male in his thirties reported that he was frustrated at not being able to "connect" with some of the Filipino males who were in their twenties:

> I was having problems talking to these guys. I like them and want to be closer friends with them, but they seemed uncomfortable around me. I brought it up to [an older Filipino male] and he said "you'll probably never be too close to those guys because they would probably never share anything too personal with you."

Interestingly, some of the Filipino respondents felt that it was difficult to interact with people at Messiah because they were unsure how to interact with non-Filipinos. Since they did not know how to fit them into the hierarchical *"kuya ate"* structure, they felt uncomfortable approaching non-Filipinos. One respondent described how Messiah was much different from her previous all-Filipino church in this way:

> Filipino member: At [my all-Filipino church] we were all a big family and everybody knew everybody. If new people came to church I felt like I could go to them and welcome them because I felt a part of it. But at Messiah I don't feel like I can do that. There are lots of people there that have been going there longer than I have and I've never met them. I don't know how to get to know them even though I'm an extrovert.
>
> Interviewer: why do you think it's different at Messiah from [your other church]?
>
> Filipino member: Since [the other church] is a Filipino church, there is already a structure there that you can fit into. You know, the older people are your *kuyas* and *ates* and you know how to fit in with them. At Messiah, you don't know how to interact with people because they come from different backgrounds, so it's hard to know how to approach people.

Another Filipino member expressed discomfort in relating to members of other ethnicities:

> It's just hard to relate. Sometimes conversations become just a "hi" and a "bye" at church because you don't know what more to talk about with people who are different from you.

Another frequently mentioned difference in interaction was how Filipinos and white Americans express conflict and disagreement. Filipinos saw whites as being more direct and confrontational that Filipinos, who preferred to address conflict more carefully or indirectly. One woman who grew up in the Philippines expressed it this way:

> Filipinos avoid people who are too direct or too offensive, so those people who offend them feel invisible. There are a lot of issues that need to be addressed that don't get addressed. [Filipinos] want to ignore it. It's frustrating for people who are direct and want to talk about these things. I'll give you an example. When Lynne [a white woman] was leading the Sunday school ministry, she would ask me, "can you teach Sunday school this week?" Whereas a Filipino would say, "I know you're busy and tired, so if you can't that's OK." So Lynne asks me that question and I say that I can't because of work or I'm tired or something, then I feel bad because I'm the one saying no. And then if I say no, she'll say "well how about next week?" For a Filipino that's an awful position to put someone in, because it makes them feel bad for saying no. Filipinos have a hard time saying no. You have to give people an out. So after someone does that to you, you just avoid them, and so Lynne feels invisible to the Filipinos.

It is difficult to assess how much each of these differences in interaction contributes to the problem of connecting socially across racial lines. However, it is clear from the frequency and intensity of responses that these differences all create obstacles to developing a sense of community and belonging among members at this church. It is also clear that the numerical minority groups bear the greatest relational costs of being in this diverse congregation.

Divided by Small Groups

Like many evangelical churches, Messiah has a large number of small group Bible studies and discussion groups. These groups serve as places to get to know other members more deeply, to pray for each other, and to learn more about the Bible or about a particular topic relevant to their spiritual lives through discussion. Messiah promotes these groups as the primary way to experience community, since it is difficult to connect with

TABLE 2.3
Ethnic Composition of Small Group Ministries

Small Group	Number of Filipinos	Number of Non-Filipinos	% Filipino
Married Couples 1	4	4	50
Married Couples 2	0	8	0
Married Couples 3	7	1	88
Married Couples 4	6	2	75
Women's Group 1	8	2	80
Women's Group 2	1	4	20
Justice/Compassion	2	7	22
Spiritual Discplines	1	5	17
Song of Solomon	5	2	71
Men's Group	3	0	100

people in a large group setting or at the Sunday morning services. The elders, therefore, see these groups as the solution to the oft-mentioned problem of social isolation at the church.

It appears, however, that the small groups at Messiah actually function to preserve the divide between Filipino and non-Filipino members. Table 2.3 shows that at this church, seventy-four members (more than half of the congregation) are involved in small groups. It also reveals that these groups are highly segregated—some groups are predominantly Filipino, and others are predominantly non-Filipino. The non-Filipino groups are quite diverse in terms of ethnicity, while the Filipino groups are mostly homogeneous. The only group that roughly approximates the ethnic composition of the church is one of the married couples groups. In the two married couples groups that are primarily Filipino, the only non-Filipino members of these groups are married to Filipino members of the group.

One of the problems with getting a more diverse mix of people in these small groups is the method of recruiting members into them. The leaders of the small groups are given the responsibility to recruit members of their groups. As a result, many leaders simply recruit friends who are already close to them. The small groups ministries thus reinforce the tendency of Filipinos to have closer ties within the church than non-Filipinos. Non-Filipinos, on the other hand, end up in groups where solidarity is less developed and more difficult to produce because of the diverse environment. While non-Filipinos may eventually experience some intimacy in these groups, the gap in intimacy experienced between Filipinos and non-Filipinos in the church probably grows wider because of the relative ease of interaction in the homogeneous Filipino groups compared to the diverse groups.

Connecting to God through Worship

On a Sunday morning, worshipers enter the hexagon-shaped multipurpose room of the elementary school; this room serves as Messiah's sanctuary. The lights are dim and the music is loud. Three young Filipino women and one young Latino woman are up front singing slow, heartfelt ballads to God into microphones with their eyes closed. They are accompanied by a young Filipino man playing acoustic guitar, a white male playing conga drums, and a young Chinese-American man playing electric bass guitar. The band plays a number of slow "soft-rock" choruses singing of their love for God and their need for God's salvation. They repeat the choruses slowly in a way that produces a mood of calm reflection. The words to the songs are projected onto a large screen at the front of the room. The congregation, standing in front of their chairs, which are arranged in a semicircle facing the band, sways to the music; some sing loudly with their hands raised, palms upward, while others bow their heads in prayer with their eyes closed.

When the worship service began at 10:30 a.m., only a few members of the congregation were present. The congregation trickles in slowly throughout this first half hour of "worship time," and by the time the worship leader closes at 11:10 with a long prayer asking God to prepare their hearts for the sermon, most of the 120 or so members of the congregation are present. As the worship band members unplug their instruments and sit down, Eddie walks up to the podium, bows his head, and asks God to speak through him to the congregation. He then begins his forty-five-minute sermon.

This is not unlike what would be seen at many young white evangelical churches on Sunday mornings all over America. Most Filipino evangelical churches, in the United States and in the Philippines, look very similar to white evangelical churches in terms of music and preaching styles. In fact, because of the influence of American evangelical missionaries, many young evangelical congregations all over the world use American-style "contemporary" soft-rock worship music and a thirty- to forty-five-minute Bible-based sermon as the main components of a Sunday church service. So for both those who grew up in mostly Filipino Protestant churches and those accustomed to white evangelical churches, the format and style of the service are familiar and comfortable.

A majority of white, Filipino, and Hispanic church members we interviewed mentioned both the worship music and Eddie's preaching as things they enjoyed about the church.

> I like the contemporary worship. It's heartfelt for me because it's the kind of music I'm accustomed to. If we worshipped using hymnals, it wouldn't be as heartfelt for me because I don't relate to that kind of music. (White)

> I like Eddie's messages. He's straightforward. He pretty much gets in your face. He's not condescending. He has a stimulating approach. (Filipino)

> Eddie's sermons are really on the mark, they are appropriate and they speak to people. He knows his audience. (Hispanic)

Interestingly, however, the African Americans we interviewed were less enthusiastic about the Sunday services, including the worship and preaching. One African American woman felt that she couldn't connect to God during the worship time:

> I get frustrated with the worship service. I have to prepare myself before I go. I have to listen to Gospel music in my car before I go in so I can get in a worshipping mindset. There's not any flexibility in the worship. You just have a set time for the songs and there's no room for the Spirit to work. The style is really inflexible too. I feel like I'm at a rock concert— or alternative or whatever. . . . I feel like we stop the work that the Holy Spirit does sometimes. Worship should be a healing time. People go into church, and come out the same, without being changed. We pray, but we don't intercede for people. We don't let God use us for each other. (African American)

Other African American members expressed a lack of connection between the preaching in the pulpit and what is going on in the community around the church:

> I was talking to [another church member] about this, and we were saying that Asian and white churches don't talk issues going on in the com-

munity. African American churches will talk about the kid that got shot last week. They talk about things happening in people's lives. (African American)

The preaching is different from what I'm used to. The church that I went to was more poor to middle-class. Poor churches talk about different things than white and Asian churches. It's good to do Biblical exegesis, but you have to speak to people. There are people whose weeks have been hell. You need to speak to those people. We need to be holistic. Address social issues, politics, things that affect people's lives. There are a lot of hurting people in the church. We need more than exegesis for hurting people. We have to meet those needs. (African American)

As Emerson and Smith (2000) argue, African American evangelical churches emphasize the community aspects of the Christian faith, such as social justice and community involvement, more than white evangelical churches, which tend to emphasize a personal relationship with God and one-on-one human relationships. Thus, to the extent that majority-Asian evangelical churches mirror their white evangelical counterparts, it would logically follow that African Americans will not relate as well to their worship and preaching styles.

Filipino vs. Anglo Time

One particular aspect of the church service that was frustrating to many white members was the issue of time. In the early years of the church white members frequently complained of the lack of punctuality in the way the service was run. Typically, the service would start five to ten minutes after the official starting time, and even then most of the church would be empty, except for a few white members of the church. The church had no "ending time" at that time and could end anywhere from 12:00 to 12:45 depending on what activities went on during the service. Both Filipino and non-Filipino members joked that the church runs on "Filipino time"—a reference to a more relaxed view of time than typically exists among white Americans. In response to complaints from some white members, however, the elders of the church decided that the service would start at 10:30 regardless of who was present, and would try to end around 12:00, although they stopped short of setting an offi-cial ending time. This policy was appreciated by many of the white members, but many still complained that the service started late some-times, ended late, and not many people were there to start worshiping at 10:30.

> I'm frustrated that the church starts late, and people show up late. That's a sign of disrespect, like church isn't important. (White)

> The service is too long. Especially if you are teaching Sunday school. I keep thinking, "It's not over yet!" (White)

> It's too casual. There's no sense of respect. There's no sense that this is church. People come in late, bring drinks in, put their feet up on the chairs. There's no sense that this is the house of God. (White)

Some members also complained that other activities, such as small group Bible studies, always started late and lasted too long.

> I liked the way that [white leader] organized the marriage group. He was hard-core about the time. It wasn't like the other groups I've been in that run on "Filipino time." He said "we're going to start at 7:30 and finish at 8:30 whether you're here or not." In other groups I've been in, people come at 9 and it ends up lasting forever. (White)

Other members, however, were upset with the new effort at punctuality. Many felt that timing everything so rigidly was "squelching the Spirit." Some leaders involved in the music worship complained that they felt like they had to stop worshipping even if God's Spirit was telling them to keep going. Others complained that there is no time for prayer during the ser-vice. So interestingly, some people at the church think that a lack of punc-tuality shows disrespect for God, while others think that having the ser-vice rigidly scheduled shows disrespect for God. This cultural difference was being framed in spiritual terms by both sides of the debate, each side claiming that their preferred style is more conducive to worshipping God.

The timing of the Sunday service continues to be an issue of contention in the church. Currently, a white member is in charge of organizing the service, and has stepped up the effort to start and end on time. This has many members happy, but others are more upset at the escalating level of rigidity in the service.

Structure and Organization

A central point of conflict at Messiah is the extent to which the church and its programs need to be organized and structured. Eddie's original vision of enabling everyone to be involved in and to contribute to the ministries of the church led to a relatively unstructured organization. Most predominantly white evangelical churches have deacons, elders, and appointed committees or leaders in charge of different aspects of church life—such as Sunday school for the kids, overseas missions, music worship, community outreach, and caring for the sick and needy. For the first year and a half of Messiah's existence, the only formal structure that existed was that there was one person in charge of music worship and one person in charge of Sunday school ministries, one person in charge of getting food for the congregation after the service, and one person in charge of announcements. Any other programs or activities that emerged did so spontaneously—by people taking the initiative to start a Bible study group, say, or an outreach ministry to the community. As a result, many programs began and ended without much consistency. After a year and a half of existence, Messiah formed an elder board, consisting of Eddie and three other men. Still, there was no formal structure designed to start and maintain programs and ministries.

While many of the respondents we interviewed were frustrated with the lack of organization, it was clear that this bothered the non-Filipino members more it did than the Filipinos.

> When the elders shared their [ideas] about getting people to help out, I felt like there was too little structure and it was too disorganized, so it's hard to know how to help. I felt powerless to help because there wasn't enough structure for me to get involved. (White)

> I don't like that if there's going to be a ministry you have to start it yourself. I have a lot of ideas about ministries, but I don't know how to start one, and I don't know if it's just me who has this passion or if others have it too. So it's hard to start something yourself. . . . And the small groups. I don't know what they are, what times they are, or how to get

involved. We need more organization . . . the hardest thing for me is the non-structuredness of our church. (African American)

It is difficult to say whether this debate over organization is a result of cultural differences. Some all-Filipino churches are very structured, with lots of committees and leaders overseeing different aspects of church life. Likewise, some white churches have very little formal structure. On average, however, it was the non-Filipinos, and whites in particular, that complained more frequently and seemed most frustrated by the lack of structure and organization in the church.

Family Time

About two years after the church began, a white member of the elder board felt the growing sense of social isolation among many of the non-Filipino members. Every few months, the church has informal meetings called "family times" where members can express new ideas for the church as well as frustrations with the way things are going. This particular elder felt that devoting an entire family time to the issue of ethnic diversity and how it affects the church would be a good idea. This became the meeting described at the beginning of this book. The church leadership up to that point had never publicly addressed the issue of ethnic diversity, either from the pulpit or in leadership meetings. Because the church continued to grow both in numbers and in diversity, it was assumed by the leadership that there were no problems in that area.

Approximately thirty members attended the "family time" meeting devoted to ethnic diversity. The majority who came were non-Filipino. The white elder who called the meeting asked four people of different backgrounds to openly share their experiences at Messiah. This led to an outpouring of heartfelt sharing about the difficulties different people experienced at the church. The discussion covered a wide range of topics, from relational isolation to the way the church was run. As we saw, a Filipina member expressed her perception that while the church was diverse in terms of demographics, it was not functionally multi-ethnic in the sense of equally valuing and incorporating different cultures into the way the church operated; and an African American member shared her feelings of discomfort during worship and said that she could not express herself during worship the way she would like to because of the worship style at the church. A number of people said that they felt socially isolated and that they didn't fit in. A Filipino member said that he was put off by what he called the "Filipino cliques" at the church, which weren't reaching out to others. A number of white members expressed their displeasure at the relaxed attitude toward time at church services and meetings. One white person shared that he was frustrated that the white people wanted the service run their way and weren't flexible on the issue of time. This frank, open dialogue continued for more than two hours.

This outpouring clearly had the feeling of a dam having finally broken. Eddie and the other two Filipino elders seemed blindsided by the level of frustration expressed at the meeting. Eddie and Ben, another Filipino elder who often preaches and who had just started as a part-time staff member at the church, both openly apologized to the group, saying that they had not known there was so much dissatisfaction at the church. Ben added that "it might seem like we don't care, but it's just that we didn't know." The meeting ended with a long prayer time, where many of those present prayed out loud that God would unify them and that these problems could be overcome. Others prayed that God would help the church defeat the "spiritual stronghold" that was being used by Satan to try to divide the church.

The sharing time and the prayer afterward seemed to have a cathartic effect. People were clearly emotionally drained after the long meeting, and a number of people hugged each other affectionately, while others embraced each other somewhat uncomfortably. The room eventually lightened up with laughter and small talk as people began to trickle out.

The conversations we had with people following this meeting were interesting. Many of those who attended the meeting were relieved and encouraged that they had been able to express their feelings openly. They were hopeful that this dialogue could continue, that church members could learn from each other, and that the more open communication would lead to meaningful change.

Many of the Filipinos, however, were clearly surprised by the level of frustration expressed. One Filipino in a leadership position said, "I had no idea we had racial problems at the church. Everything seemed to be going so well." The elders were not only surprised by the level of discontent expressed at the meeting, but also very discouraged because they had no idea what they might do about it. Some Filipino members were clearly defensive. Some said that they did not feel like they fit in at the church either and were puzzled that people were turning it into a Filipino vs. non-

Filipino conflict. They felt they were being unfairly blamed for the problems others were having, when they were having the same problems themselves. Others felt that the church shouldn't be focusing on cultural issues—things that divide us—but should focus on doing what the Bible says, worshiping God and telling others about Jesus.

This "family time" meeting was something of a watershed moment for the church. At the next elders' meeting the elders decided that they needed to be much more intentional about the way they were doing things. They met every week for the next few months and came up with a "vision statement" with six core values meant to define the direction the church should go in the future. One of those six values was "reconciliation," which they defined as working intentionally to overcome divisions created by age, gender, ethnicity, and economic status. Several Sunday morning sermons in the few months following that meeting focused on being reconciled and overcoming racial divisions.

Despite this initial recognition that change needed to happen, and some initial steps taken toward change, relatively few public dialogues have taken place since that meeting that address the racial and cultural diversity of the church. One that did occur was one year after that initial meeting, when a number of people in the church decided that they wanted to have a "reconciliation workshop" at the annual weekend-long church retreat. The leadership agreed, and a three-hour meeting was held at the conference center in which a multiracial group of members performed skits illustrating various tensions within the church that arise from their different backgrounds. This was followed by a panel discussion in which people from different backgrounds talked about how they experience friendship, and then small group discussions centered on the issues raised.

This workshop produced many of the same reactions prompted by the initial family time meeting. Some members expressed relief that the issues were being discussed and that an open dialogue was continuing. Others felt defensive, concerned that Filipinos were being singled out as responsible for the problems, or that it was not wise for a church to focus on these problems rather than on what they feel are the central tasks of the church.

Since that retreat, public statements or discussions concerning the racial and ethnic diversity of the church have grown even more infrequent. A number of the members who were initially hopeful about the possibilities for change have become disillusioned. A few have left the church. The effects of those meetings, however, have continued. As a result of the six core values being clearly stated, the church has become much more structured and organized, with appointed leaders and teams in charge of promoting each of the six values. However, not much has happened to promote the "reconciliation" value. Time schedules for the Sunday morning services and meetings are more strictly followed. A number of highly organized white members have emerged into leadership positions. Some members of the church, particularly white members, are very encouraged by these changes. Others, however, have expressed that these are not the kinds of changes they were looking for. Many in this latter group wonder if the church is becoming too rigid and bureaucratic. Still others wonder whether the church is becoming more culturally white, and why the values of punctuality and organization are beginning to take precedence over other values. Indeed, the church seems to be drawing more white members. The Filipino percentage is still around half. It appears that the representation of other ethnic groups—African, African American, Chinese, Korean, and Hispanic—may be dwindling. It has been a long time since a public forum was held where it would be possible to raise these concerns.

Learning from This Case

In our reflecting on the interviews we conducted and the prolonged contact we had with this congregation, a number of interesting racial dynamics emerged that we want to highlight. We also want to keep them in mind when considering our other five cases, in order to determine whether these are simply unique to this particular church, or if they might be characteristic of interracial religious groups in general.

Spiritual enrichment as a result of diversity. Nearly all of the people we interviewed, regardless of ethnic group membership, saw much benefit to being in an interracial congregation. Most notably, all but a few respondents mentioned that the diversity of the church was either a main reason for coming to the church, or one of the main things they enjoyed about the church. Many respondents stated their appreciation for the congregation's diversity in theological terms, saying that it is a more "biblical" than homogeneous church, and that it is a true representation of heaven on earth.

In addition, many of those interviewed who were experiencing high levels of frustration and difficulty told us that they would never consider going back to a homogeneous church. The members we interviewed who had left the church because of social isolation were either attending or looking for another interracial church. It seems that for many of the congregants of this church, the value they have placed on worshiping in a diverse congregation is so high that they have simply ruled out the option of returning to a homogeneous congregation.

Relational isolation among numerical minority group members. The most striking pattern in our in-depth interviews was the difference in Filipinos' and non-Filipinos' reports about their experience in forming friendships and feeling a sense of belonging in the church. Specifically, most non-Filipinos appeared to be struggling to find and develop any close ties within the congregation.

It appears that in the case of this church, the social isolation of members of numerical minority groups (Anglos, Hispanics, African Americans, Koreans) is not a result of intentional discrimination or exclusion, but rather a combination of cultural and intraorganizational dynamics. First of all, many of the original Filipino members of this church have built-in social networks from previous friendships and family connections. These networks are difficult for outsiders to break into. This probably happens in monoethnic churches as well—central members of any organization tend to have denser social ties that leave peripheral members feeling left out. There is a definite ethnic effect here, however, illustrated by the greater number and strength of friendship ties among the Filipino church members as compared to the non-Filipino members (see tables 2.1 and 2.2). It is also illustrative that many of the original non-Filipino members, who were close friends with Eddie during his college days, have left the church. Most of the original Filipino members still attend.

Religiously powered ethnocentrism. Because this is a religious organization where members interpret most of life through a religiously informed grid, differences in culture are often talked about in absolute terms. This phenomenon is illustrated through the debate over the way the church service is timed. Time-oriented white members viewed the lax timing of the church service not only as inconvenient for them, but also as a sign of disrespect toward God. Likewise, those who preferred a more flexible schedule felt that rigidly timing a service was squelching the Holy Spirit. Framing this cultural issue in absolute terms raises the stakes considerably, producing more conflict and less opportunity for compromise on issues of differing cultural values.

Furthermore, all religious expression is embedded in particular cultural forms, so individuals experience God through culturally specific media. In evangelical Protestantism, worship music is a key component of "connecting to God" in a church service. Thus, differences in musical preference and worship style get framed in absolute terms. This raises the stakes in conflicts over music styles and forms of expression, as each group feels their particular style is more conducive to "connecting to God" or to "being transformed" by the experience.

Whites in the minority. This case is interesting because white people were in the minority, both in numbers and in leadership positions. This is often not the case in interracial organizations. It appears to us that the leadership of Messiah may have taken the complaints of white members more seriously than those of other ethnic groups. This was reflected in the move toward a more rigid time structure, which was pushed for by whites more heavily than by other groups. It could be that this was because whites are the largest of the numerical minority groups at Messiah, or because the one non-Filipino elder at this church was white.

Another explanation could be that the white members of this church are much more likely to continually push the leadership for the changes they want, and much more likely to move into leadership positions that are conducive to effecting change. Three out of the four elders at the church are Filipino, and most of the members in charge of specific ministries, such as Sunday school and worship music, are also Filipino. However, a few key positions are now occupied by highly organized whites, including one who is in charge of coordinating all of the different ministries together, and one who is in charge of scheduling and coordinating the entire Sunday service. These two members have had a tremendous influence on the form and the structure the church takes.

It could be that this was just an accident—that these two highly motivated members just happened to be in the right place at the right time to give the church some of the structure that many members of all ethnicities wanted. Or it could be that whites, because they are culturally dominant in the larger society and are likely to be in leadership positions in their secular professions, feel more comfortable demanding the changes they want and moving into leadership positions to make those changes. It could also be that the numerical majority group members in leadership, in this case Filipinos, are more likely to value the opinions of whites as opposed to other groups because of the culturally dominant position of whites in the larger society. As one member stated, "since this church is in America, it should go by 'American' standards."

Overall, this case shows that there are a number of conflicts and obstacles that can arise from racial diversity in a small congregation. It is interesting because the ethnic group that is the numerical majority in numbers and in leadership is not the majority in the larger society. The experience of this congregation suggests that numerical minorities within a racially diverse organization bear the highest relational costs. It also appears, however, that whites receive some benefits within an organization even if they are a numerical minority because of their dominant position in the larger society. These benefits may include a greater likelihood of having their concerns heard and a greater likelihood of moving into leadership positions.

Another interesting aspect of this case is its small size in absolute numbers. This may produce more social isolation for numerical minorities than would be the case in large congregation, since the absolute numbers for each minority group are fairly small.

Despite the high costs they incurred, however, many members of the numerical minority of this church are committed to staying and are spiritually enriched by the interracial environment. The fact that those who left because of social isolation are not considering going to a racially homogeneous church suggests that experiencing diversity in worship, for some, changes a person spiritually to such an extent that worshiping in a homogeneous setting becomes unthinkable, even in the face of high costs. This finding suggests that religious organizations may have resources that secular organizations do not have to overcome the social forces that produce segregation. On the other hand, this case suggests that religious organizations may have difficulties that secular organizations do not have in creating understanding and compromise among ethnic groups. The religiously powered ethnocentrism we observed clearly makes compromise and understanding between ethnic groups more difficult. In addition, connecting to God, the central project of religion, takes place through culturally specific media. Thus, it is difficult for people to feel connected to God using unfamiliar cultural forms and rituals.

Subsequent chapters describe organizations that are quite different in racial composition, history, and structure. We will attempt to keep an eye on the dynamics we found in this first case to see if they appear in other cases.

3

A Place to Call Home

Like Messiah Fellowship, Wilcrest is an evangelical church. And like Messiah, Wilcrest is an interracial congregation. But Wilcrest diverges from Messiah on many points. While Messiah is nondenominational, Wilcrest is solidly Southern Baptist, both in theology and—by virtue of its location in Houston, Texas—geographically. There are more Southern Baptists in Texas than there are people in many other states, and Houston, with nearly 750 Southern Baptist congregations, is no exception.

With average Sunday attendance running between 450 and 550 people, Wilcrest is four times the size of Messiah Fellowship. Yet the congregation considers itself small, sitting in the shadows of such behemoths as First Baptist, Second Baptist, Sagemont, and others, with their congregations numbering in the thousands and their multimillion dollar budgets. Wilcrest is a lower-middle-class congregation (in contrast to middle-class Messiah Fellowship). Its annual budget—about half a million dollars, which they often strain to meet—is less than some of the larger Baptist churches in town receive in a weekly offering. Its physical plant is decaying, the air conditioning often does not work effectively during the steamy Houston summers (which seem to last about six months), and the décor says "Hello early 1970s!" The physical appearance, however, does not keep the congregation from expanding. It has grown fairly steadily for about a decade.

Wilcrest Church has been around much longer than Messiah Fellowship. Founded in the late 1960s, its present buildings were built or modified in the early 1970s. At that time, Wilcrest was a fast-growing, all-white congregation. It continued to grow, and it stayed all white, until the mid-1980s, when the oil bust hit Houston hard and many whites left the immediate community or left Houston altogether. Through the late 1980s and early 1990s, non-whites repopulated the neighborhood. As a result, the neighborhood in which Wilcrest was located changed from nearly 100 percent white to 10 percent white in the most recent census. The neighborhood is now populated by Latinos (many of whom are immigrants), African Americans, and African, Caribbean, Vietnamese, and Chinese immigrants. Once a rising middle-class, white-collar, professional neighborhood, it is now a working-class neighborhood, filled with people who work long hours and multiple shifts.

During the changing times in the neighborhood, Wilcrest did its best to remain a white congregation, including starting mission churches for respective groups of non-whites and having cards printed up to hand to non-white visitors telling them about alternative, non-white congregations where they would feel more comfortable. These techniques were effective, but with the changes in the neighborhood the congregation declined in size, and average worship attendance dipped below 200. Something had to be done.

Around 1990, Wilcrest's then pastor wanted to sell the church buildings to another ethnic church group and move to a white neighborhood. The lay leaders, after much thought and prayer, decided they should stay put. With the pastor not feeling suited for such a challenge, a mutual decision was made for him to step down. The leaders of Wilcrest vaguely realized that their decision to stay meant they would have to open their doors to neighbors who wanted to come. So they had a general idea that the next pastor would need to know how to go about doing that. Mostly they knew they needed a pastor who was a leader and could help stabilize the church. Through a series of events, including the near hiring of someone else, they settled upon a twenty-nine-year-old preacher with a doctorate in theology and the last name of Woo. Part Chinese, part white, and married to a Mexican American, this pastor introduced a major shake-up in the congregation immediately on arriving. His driving vision was for Wilcrest to be a multi-ethnic congregation, one filled with people from around the world.

As a key first step, Pastor Woo worked with the congregation to define a vision. Over the course of months of study, meetings, and planning, they arrived at the following vision statement: "Wilcrest Baptist Church is God's multiethnic bridge, that draws all people to Jesus Christ, who transforms them from unbelievers to missionaries." This vision statement communicates the driving purposes of the congregation: to be multiethnic, to help people mature as Christians, and ultimately to be missionaries and to cross cultures, not only in faraway places, but also in the local community and inside the congregation itself. The congregation repeats the mission statement often, and it appears on the cover of every bulletin.

Through much effort, prayer, and outreach, the congregation has more than doubled in size since Pastor Woo's arrival. The impetus for this growth has been atypical. For most congregations in the United States, growth comes mainly from transfers—people moving from one congregation to another within the same denomination. Nationally, 55 percent of new members come to congregations as such transfers (U.S. Congregational Life Survey 2000). This is not true of Wilcrest. At more than three and half times the national average for U.S. congregations, a full seventy percent of Wilcrest's growth has been from what scholars define as "switchers"—people who were previously involved in different faith traditions. Members of Wilcrest include former Buddhists, animists, Catholics, and Methodists, among others. Many new Wilcrest members, especially those who came from other Christian traditions, were people who had attended a congregation on and off as children but had not been involved as adults. Another ten percent of the church's growth comes from people who can be called "first-timers," those who had never been involved in a faith tradition previously.

Through much effort, prayer, and struggle, Wilcrest has become (at least demographically) the realization of Pastor Woo's dream. A majority minority congregation, Wilcrest includes members from more than forty nations. Racially/ethnically, Wilcrest is about 42 percent white, 30 percent Latino, 20 percent black, 5 percent Asian, and 3 percent other. Within each of these categories are native-born and immigrant, and people from multiple locations. For example, among the blacks, about one-third are U.S.–born, another third are from various nations in Africa, and the remaining third are from Caribbean nations.

Despite the impressive array of racial and ethnic diversity, continued efforts to change, and a willingness on the part of staff to seek change, Wilcrest was, at the time of our interviews, still a structurally white congregation. Its worship style, leaders, staff, and committee members were overwhelmingly white. Its strong affiliation with the Southern Baptist tradition means its Sunday school materials, music, magazines, news, conferences, social networks, mentors, and heroes are closely tied to a tradition rooted in whiteness. Moreover, because the non-white growth has occurred since the early 1990s, and most of it since the late 1990s, whites have, on average, been part of Wilcrest longer than non-whites. Whites, then, remain at the center of structural power, and as the largest single racial group, they remain at the center demographically.

All of these factors make Wilcrest different from Messiah Fellowship in significant ways and provide a unique comparative case for our concerns. What are the costs and benefits of membership, and for whom, within this larger congregation, with a longer history than Messiah Fellowship and a culture of being a historically white congregation?

Why They Are There

What first attracted people to Wilcrest? Based on a written survey completed by all the adults of Wilcrest, we identified a few patterns for why people first began attending. Some first came because it was close to where they lived or worked, so they thought they would try it. Others came because a co-worker, a neighbor, a friend, a family member, or a staff member invited them (this seems to be the most common reason). Some came because they received a flyer about the church, or someone knocked on their door and encouraged them to give Wilcrest a try. Others came because their children were involved in child or youth activities at the church, and their children kept singing the praises of the place. Others heard it was a Bible-centered church with a caring pastor. Some said they were drawn to Wilcrest for reasons they could not explain specifically. Many, especially in the last few years, and especially the non-whites, said that the congregation's racial and ethnic diversity attracted them.

For our purposes, more important than why people first came to Wilcrest is why they stayed (or left) and what their experiences are in the congregation. For all groups, perhaps the most frequently mentioned reason for staying was a sense of warmth and welcoming from others. According to this man from the Caribbean islands,

> What attracted us was the warmth of the people and the love that they showed. They greet you at the door, they try to find out things about you, be friendly with you, they even visit you. At other churches we visited, people may say hello, but nothing like visiting us.

A Cuban American woman, who is married to a darker skinned South American immigrant, said, "the people were very friendly to me, and more importantly to my husband. The men embraced him, shaking his hand, welcoming our family." One of the very first non-whites to come to

Wilcrest was an African American man married to a white woman. He said he stayed because of the love he felt—"they just showered us with love," as he put it—and because he became a Christian through Pastor Woo, as did his wife after they had attended for two weeks. According to his wife, they stayed because

> when we first came, being mixed race, my husband and I, it has always been an issue when we go to group functions. The first thing you look for is acceptance, how you are perceived. When we came here, we were greeted so warmly and so lovingly. And the following Sunday, when I accepted Christ, they had us stand at the front of the sanctuary. The people came up to greet us, and I can't tell you all the kind, loving words people said. My husband and I were in awe.

Pastor Woo is also an important reason people stay. "He is a such a man of God, preaching from Scripture what it says, even if it is uncomfortable." "Pastor Woo knew my name after just one visit, and I love his preaching." Pastor Woo also has made it a practice since his arrival at Wilcrest to visit people in their homes, especially if they have recently begun attending; and he has learned enough Spanish to converse at a basic level with Spanish speakers. These efforts toward connection clearly impress people.

People also stay because their children very much want to stay, because of the programs that are offered for children and youth, and because, as so many have said, Wilcrest feels like family, like home. This latter reason cannot be overstated.

In a mobile society such as the United States, and especially in large cities such as Houston, most people are from somewhere else (another part of the country, or in Wilcrest's case, often another part of the world). Because most people are not native to the area, to find a sense of rootedness, security, a home, is a central, driving need. Most of those who have stayed at Wilcrest say it is their home, their family—a place where they feel they belong, where they know people and people know them, where they share a common purpose with others. In short—and this is part of the importance of religious congregations in the modern world—Wilcrest is community.

But whites and non-whites differ in one important respect regarding why they chose to stay at Wilcrest. Of the whites we interviewed who had been at Wilcrest since Rodney Woo's arrival (seven of the ten whites interviewed), only one mentioned that the racial and ethnic diversity was a reason that drew them to the congregation or kept them there. In stark contrast, almost all the non-whites mentioned the diversity as a reason they stayed at Wilcrest, and it was a major influence on how welcomed they felt. Here are a few typical responses from non-whites to the question of why they stayed at Wilcrest:

The different types of people. It is not just one mold, there are all different ethnic groups here. It fills a need that many people are looking for. And that helps Wilcrest, because people probably come here for that reason, enjoy it, and so they are probably more friendly and open to everyone else. (Mexican American)

When I first came in 1988, it was not diverse, and I did not feel welcomed. So I did not stay. I came back ten years later to visit, and so much had changed. I felt welcomed. There were people from around the world. And I was hungry to learn the Word in this diverse place. These are the things that kept me here. (Caribbean immigrant)

I feel comfortable here. I no speak much English, but people still welcome me. It different from my Hispanic Catholic Church, it better here. You see no only white people, no only black people, no only Hispanic people. Different peoples in the same church I think the best. (Honduran immigrant)

When I first visited I looked hard at the cover of the bulletin. It drew me in, saying this was a church for everyone. I looked up at the people in the sanctuary. They seemed to be from everywhere. It was beautiful. I felt like they said "Welcome to the family. This is your new home." And I thanked God. (African immigrant)

Clearly, being demographically multicultural is very important to the non-whites, it is in fact a major factor in feeling welcomed. We wondered, then, how it is that Wilcrest was able to become diverse, considering that the first non-whites who came would not have experienced this diversity. Given that in the beginning diversity would have been limited, and given what we know from social theory, we would expect the turnover of non-whites to be very high, as suggested by the Caribbean immigrant's first Wilcrest experience described above. We asked Pastor Rodney Woo if he saw a lot of turnover in the early years:

Absolutely. In fact, I used to tell our deacons, we have to grow by seventy or eighty new people a year just to stay the same size. For all sorts of reasons, the turnover of our non-whites was extremely high. I was recently checking on the people that joined our congregation in the first years I was here. In my first year and a half as pastor, seventy-eight non-whites were baptized into the congregation. Eight years later, only three or four of that original group are still here, and most who left left after a very short time. For the whites that joined during that period, some have left as well, but more than half are still here.

Clearly, at least in Wilcrest's case, the turnover of non-whites was very high when the percentage of non-whites was small. So how did Wilcrest become majority minority?

The answer lies in the frequency of visits by non-whites—Wilcrest has a good location on cross streets in a diverse neighborhood and eagerly invites people to visit—and in who the first non-whites were who stayed. Earlier we heard from an interracial couple—the wife white, the husband African American. MaryAnn and Glynn came to Wilcrest shortly after Rodney Woo arrived, and have been there ever since, making Glynn perhaps the longest attending non-white. Several factors are significant in this case. Glynn is more culturally assimilated to white culture than many African Americans. He is married to a white woman, and he grew up in integrated or primarily white living environments and schools because his father was in the army. He spent many of his high school years in Germany. He is politically and socially conservative (corresponding to the dominant views of the whites at Wilcrest when he first arrived). And he prefers white worship styles to black worship styles, in part because he became a Christian within a white church context, and in part because he has negative memories of occasionally attending black Pentecostal churches growing up.

His case is typical in that many of the original people who stayed wanted to be in a white church context, or, because of marriage to a white spouse, found Wilcrest to be the best fit—that is, a culturally white church that was trying to do things differently, including the vision statement posted everywhere that indicated Wilcrest's intent to be multi-ethnic. The original non-whites who stayed, then, were in some ways less free to leave Wilcrest, or had additional ties that kept them at Wilcrest rather than pulling them elsewhere, as was happening for most non-whites. This first wave of non-white stayers, though small in number, helped pave the road for second-wave non-whites. A good case in point is a Dominican man, Fernando, and his wife Lorraine, who is of Puerto Rican and European descent and was raised in the New York area. The couple arrived about two and a half years after Glynn and MaryAnn. Fernando explained that he and his wife actually left Wilcrest at one point because they did not feel welcomed. He related a particularly dramatic event that crystallized how they felt:

> Wilcrest had a mission trip planned to Canada and they asked for volunteers to drive the people to the airport. So I volunteer my van, I cleaned it up, I vacuumed it. I was like the kid looking forward to a trip to the beach; I was getting to serve. I volunteered because it used to be that if you wanted to be included, you had to try to include yourself, you had to be a servant and that was my attitude. So I get my van, I line it up in the row outside of the church, I even put the AC running so that when they get in it will be nice and cool. I'm looking forward to it. I even had loaded some of their baggage in my van.
>
> We all get in a circle, hold hands, and pray. Then it is time to get in the vans. I am excited to serve. Everybody is laughing with friends and family. They all get in vans, but nobody is getting in mine. I'm like "Hey, how about here?" But everyone got in different vans and left.
>
> There I was, left alone in the parking lot. I felt low. I felt like a nothing. It was like a kid who had candy taken away from him by a bully. I said to myself in Spanish, "You know, this is a good example of why my family shouldn't be here. We've gotta move on. We're not really welcome. Hey, they have a clique, and we're not part of it." I went home and told my wife, who was already feeling like an outsider at the church, what happened. She said, "What?! They did that? We're not going there anymore." So we left.

While Fernando's story may be more dramatic than most, the feelings of isolation and being excluded are not. And the end result—leaving—was the same as well. But because there were a few non-whites in the congregation at this point, something different happened. As Fernando tells it:

> Someone from Wilcrest called me to tell me that I had some things in the van that the Canada team needed. So I took the stuff to Glynn (the African American man noted earlier), who was my friend. When I brought the stuff to him, I broke down and I cried. And Glynn, being my friend, felt so bad. He talked to me for a long time, telling me how sorry

he was. I told him we had decided to leave, and couldn't come back. He said, "I am not giving up that easily."

He called Pastor Rodney and told him what had happened.

Pastor Rodney called me right away. I told him I couldn't talk to him now. I told him my family was going to try other churches, and after we did we could talk.

So we go to another church, and I couldn't believe what the sermon was about. The preacher said, "Some of you are being sensitive, some of you are hurt by things and want to run away, because you are looking sideways. You have to look up. Persevere. Ask God for strength to change things for the better." I mean, it was a message that God spoke to me. And Cynthia and I said, let's let Pastor Rodney come talk to us.

Pastor Rodney came right away, we met, and he apologized for what happened. I told him, I said, "Pastor Rodney, what I think is, I think we're going back." But I also said, "We need to analyze the situation. There are too many cliques here. The goldfish are going with the goldfish and the tropical fish are with the tropical fish. We gotta be inclusive."

So through the help of Glynn, the persistence of Pastor Rodney, and a timely sermon, Fernando's family returned to Wilcrest. And Fernando returned with a passion to see Wilcrest become more welcoming to non-whites.

Since his return, Fernando has greatly expanded the Spanish ministry. This ministry includes a Spanish-speaking adult Sunday school class, which he usually teaches. He has taught Spanish speakers English in formal classes held at the church. To help non-Spanish-speaking people go on mission trips to Central and South America, he has taught Spanish classes to English speakers at the church. He also arranged to have the worship services translated into Spanish, so that Spanish-speaking immigrants could come to Wilcrest and feel like they belong. With the help of the Spanish Sunday school class, the church raised the funds to purchase translation equipment, which includes translation packs and earphones. With this equipment, Fernando, or one of the others he has trained, can sit in a different room, watch the service on a television feed through a video camera, hear the service through earphones, and simultaneously translate what they hear into Spanish for the Spanish speakers in the congregation who have taken one of the translation packs as they entered the sanctuary.

Fernando and the other Spanish speakers have had to do the work to see these inclusive mechanisms begin and continue. The leadership at

Wilcrest has supported the ideas and the principles, but has found it difficult to commit significant material resources. Fernando and other Hispanics, and a few others who joined them along the way, have had to find creative ways to secure the resources and to build the ministries. But these efforts have done a great deal to draw non-Whites, especially Latinos, to Wilcrest. They have meant that parents who have limited English or who desire community with others from Latin countries can come to Wilcrest and feel like they have found a home, and their children, usually fluent in English, can feel like they have found a home as well.

Wilcrest, then, has benefited from the fact that some of the first wave of non-whites who came there were interracially married or were seeking a white worship service. For these people, the forces pulling them to Wilcrest were strong enough to keep them there, at least for a significant period of time. They in turn helped retain a greater proportion of second-wave people, some of whom decided they would commit themselves to helping Wilcrest diversify. Wilcrest also benefited from frequent visits by non-whites, generated by its location and its many active outreach events. Thus, even if the turnover of non-whites was high, the significant number of non-white visitors made Wilcrest appear more racially diverse than its membership was, and thus increased the likelihood that the next wave would stay. Turnover of non-whites has now declined dramatically; it is now no higher than that for whites.

Friendships

In chapter 2, we found that the largest group in the Messiah congregation—Filipinos—had a higher percentage of same-race friends than did other groups in the congregation. We also saw that Filipinos, relative to other groups in the congregation, were more likely to say their closest friends were within the congregation. As we noted earlier in this chapter, Wilcrest differs from Messiah in size, in the race of the largest group, in location, and in average socioeconomic status of its members. Given the differences between Messiah Fellowship and Wilcrest, do we find a similar pattern?

As at Messiah, we asked the Wilcrest people we interviewed for the first names of their three closest friends in the church. We also asked them for the first names of their three closest friends outside of church. After we had written down the names, we asked them if they were closer to friend one in the church or friend one outside the church. We repeated this question for friends two and three. Once we had asked these questions, we named each friend and asked for their race/ethnicity. We interviewed twenty-six Wilcrest people, chosen in proportions intended to approximate those in the congregation—ten whites, nine Latinos, and seven blacks. The Latinos we selected represented six nationalities, and five of the nine were foreign-born. The blacks we selected represented five nationalities, and four of the seven were foreign-born.

Though not the majority, the largest and most influential racial group at Wilcrest is the whites. If we are to find the same pattern at Wilcrest as at Messiah, whites should have a higher percentage of same-race friends than other groups. Table 3.1 presents our findings. Whether we examine the relationship one friendship at a time, or compare the overall means of the race of people's three closest friends, the conclusion is the same: whites are both statistically and substantively more likely to have friends of the same race than are non-whites. On average, 2.7 of whites' top three friends at Wilcrest are white. In contrast, for non-whites, an average of 1.56 of the three closest friends were of the same race, meaning that nearly half of non-whites' closest friends are people from racial groups other than their own.

As yet another indicator of the disparity reflected in Table 3.1, when we compared the names of the three closest friends, we occasionally found a non-white including a white person whom we had also interviewed. We would then go to the friendship list of that white person to see if it included the non-white person who named them as one of their three closest friends. We did not find any matches. In other words, although non-whites nominated whites as their closest friends, the corresponding whites, while likely counting that non-white person as a friend, did not name that person in their top three. This result suggests that the depth of friendships at Wilcrest for whites is deeper than for non-whites.

If Wilcrest whites have deeper friendships at Wilcrest than do non-whites, we would expect that their closest friends are inside Wilcrest, rather than outside. As Table 3.2 shows, this is indeed the case. In only one instance did a white person claim to have a closer friend outside the church than within the church. Indeed, during this portion of the interview, whites often had great difficulty even thinking of friends outside of Wilcrest. As one man said, "Wilcrest is my family and my home. I know people at work and other places, but they are really just acquaintances. Because we have different value systems, I wouldn't be able share with them what I truly am thinking and feeling."

TABLE 3.1
Percentage of Wilcrest Members' Closest Friends
Who Are the Same Race as the Respondent (n = 26)

	Non-White Members	White Members
#1 church friend same race	38	80*
#2 church friend same race	50	90*
#3 church friend same race	25	100**
Mean # of 3 closest friends who are the same race	1.56	2.70**

NOTES: Pearson's Chi-Square test (+ p < .1, * p < .05, ** p < .01)

Non-whites, however, are about equally likely to say their closest friends are outside the church as that they are inside the church. Whereas whites on average claimed 2.9 out of 3 close friends were within the church, the average for non-whites in the sample was 1.7 out of 3. Interestingly, in our sample, non-whites appear more likely to find one close friend inside the church (63 percent say their closest friend is inside the church) than a second or third (for the third closest friend, half say the friend is outside the church).

But the Wilcrest results present us with an interpretation problem. Though the differences we see in the tables above may be a result of differences in group size and position within the congregation, they could also be traced to the fact that whites, on average, have been at Wilcrest longer than non-whites. The whites in our sample have been at Wilcrest an average of 9.8 years, while non-whites have been at Wilcrest an average of just 3.5 years. Given that friendships take time to develop, this difference could explain our findings.

We have a couple of ways to examine the role of time. Four of the whites in our sample have been at Wilcrest ten years or more. When we

TABLE 3.2
Analysis of Location of Closest Friends for Wilcrest Members
(n = 26)—Inside the Church or Outside the Church?

	Non-White	White
#1 closest friend is inside church	63	100*
#2 closest friend is inside church	56	90+
# 3 closest friend is inside church	50	100**
Mean # of 3 closest friends who are inside church	1.69	2.90**

NOTES: Pearson's Chi-Square test (+ p < .1, * p < .05, ** p < .01)

remove them, the average time at Wilcrest for whites drops to 5.8 years. Comparing the remaining whites to non-whites on the questions summarized in Tables 3.1 and 3.2 produces the same findings. Whites are more likely to have close friends who are of their own race, and are more likely to say that their closest friends are inside rather than outside the church.

Yet this comparison still leaves us with a longer average time at Wilcrest for whites than for non-whites, so it is not a conclusive test. There are simply too few whites and non-whites in our sample who overlap in length of time at Wilcrest to conduct any meaningful comparisons. So we cannot answer the question of time versus group size and centrality with this approach.

But it might be useful to compare Blacks and Hispanics, as they too differ in proportion to the overall group size and in centrality. Because of the efforts of Fernando and others, Latino participation and membership at Wilcrest has grown substantially—Latinos account for nearly a third of the congregation at the time of this writing (compared to about 20 percent for blacks). Because there are Spanish ministries, and perhaps because the senior pastor's wife is Hispanic, Hispanics are (or appear to be) more core to Wilcrest than do black members in terms of size and influence.

At the same time, the average Hispanic in our sample has been at Wilcrest for a somewhat shorter time than has the average black in our sample (3.2 years for Hispanics compared to 3.7 years for blacks). If time is the key factor, then we would expect blacks to be slightly more likely than Latinos to say their closest friends are within rather than outside the congregation, or at least not *less* likely to have close friends inside the congregation. But in fact we find the opposite. Latinos report, on average, that 2 of their 3 closest friends are inside the congregation, compared to 1.3 out of 3 for blacks. More research is needed to corroborate this finding, but the research here suggests patterns similar to those we found at Messiah—that numerical minorities are less likely to have their closest friends within the church, and less likely to have same-race close friendships within the church.

Leaving Wilcrest

For many years, Wilcrest has held "exit interviews" with people who have decided to leave. The purpose of these interviews is simply to ask why the people are leaving, so that Wilcrest as a congregation can become a better place for others. Pastor Woo shared with us the main reasons he hears in these interviews. In addition, we interviewed a few people who had left prior to the time of our interview and a few who have left since, and we draw from these sources as well.

Like many congregations, the most common reason people give for leaving is that they are moving. With many apartment complexes in the few-mile radius around Wilcrest, moving is common. Some people with the transportation means move and continue to travel to Wilcrest (some coming from forty miles or so away), but most people living in apartments find the transportation and time constraints too burdensome. In the past, non-whites have been more likely to move than whites, but more recently this has evened out, for at least two reasons. Some of the whites at Wilcrest are reaching retirement age and are consequently leaving Houston (and therefore Wilcrest). Meanwhile, with the growing racial and ethnic diversity at Wilcrest and an increased sense of belonging, a number of non-whites told us that they have decided not to move in order to stay closer to the church; or if they have moved, they have chosen a new location that still allows them to attend.

As this reasoning suggests, moving can be the key reason, or just *a* reason to give for leaving. For example, at each step in Wilcrest's process of becoming more interracial, a few whites have moved and left the church. Some left when the decision was made to stay in the neighborhood. Some left when Pastor Woo came. Some left when an African American youth minister was hired (he has since left). When we asked Pastor Woo if people left when the youth minister came because they thought he wasn't qualified or because of prejudice, he said "I think it was prejudice. They would never say that. They would say, you know, 'we're gonna move to a better school.' We have people who are commuting thirty or forty miles away to the church so moving ten miles out, it's hard to see that moving was the primary reason. I think they never bought into the vision."

We interviewed a white member who had been attending Wilcrest since 1972 and had been a deacon since the late 1970s. We asked him how he felt about the changes at the church:

> I think it is a good thing that our church is open to everybody. But I don't really understand why we have to, well, talk about it all the time. Open the doors and whoever comes comes. It shouldn't matter what

color you are. I am a big supporter of this church. I have been visiting people and inviting them to come to church for over twenty years. I am delighted to see the church grow. But I must say, if our worship changes much more, I will be embarrassed to invite others to come. The pace of some of the music, the loudness, it is just not right. I alternate between being sad and mad. Anyone is welcome at our church, but when they start changing the worship, that is when it has gone too far. Honestly, I don't know how many more changes my wife and I can handle. People have left because of the changes. If we keep moving away from reverential hymns and keep talking about multi-ethnic this, multi-ethnic that, my wife and I may be the next to go. And that would be a sad day for us. We have given our lives to this church.

When this man and his wife left the church a year and half after our interview, the official reason given was that he had decided to retire early and they were moving away from Houston. Our earlier interview with him, however, reveals the complexity of the relationship between moving and membership in the church. The thoughts he expressed during the interview would suggest that at least part of the decision to move was motivated by what he and his wife felt about the church. They viewed what used to be their church as becoming someone else's church.

As Pastor Woo said, no one tells him at the exit interview that they are leaving because they are prejudiced. But his opinion is that some do indeed leave for this reason. For example, one white family, the father a professional with an advanced degree, joined Wilcrest well after the church had become racially and ethnically diverse. After a couple of years, they left. The father told Pastor Woo that they were leaving because they did not feel like the youth group offered his children what they needed. He felt the kinds of kids in the youth group did not provide the best environment for his teenagers to learn and develop. He assured Pastor Woo it was not the racial diversity that was the problem; rather, he expressed an opinion that many of the kids in the youth group tended to be people who were loud, who came from rougher neighborhoods, and who placed a lower value on education.

The non-whites who left, especially in the earlier years, gave reasons such as struggling to fit in, feeling like they didn't belong, or wanting to attend a congregation with their relatives or friends. Moreover, because many of the non-whites were new to the faith, had inconsistent or ove___, demanding work schedules, or suffered severe family problems, they occasionally simply disappeared, unable to attend.

Many people we or Pastor Woo talked to, whether white or non-white, but especially the non-whites, left "infected" with being in an interracial congregation. Just as those we interviewed who currently attend Wilcrest say they could not imagine ever again being apart of a homogeneous congregation, so those who left (except for whites such as those mentioned above and a few African Americans) had hopes of finding another interracial congregation. As one congregant put it, "We are never going to be the same once we have encountered the truly interracial experience. It is experiencing God in such a bigger way." As we saw, this feeling was true of Messiah Fellowship as well.

Racial Diversity: Much to Celebrate, and a Few Difficulties

We asked Wilcrest people what they thought about the services, their joys at the church, what frustrations they had, and what they thought about the racial diversity. Nearly all of the non-whites mentioned racial diversity among their joys and what they loved about the services. With two exceptions, none of the whites volunteered any opinions or comments on the racial diversity of the congregation, although when we asked specific questions about it they too spoke in very positive terms.

In short, everyone we interviewed at Wilcrest liked the racial diversity, appreciated it, and even was infected by it. People told us that the racial diversity added flavor, spice, variety, excitement, meaning, enrichment, depth, and beauty. One white male, the only white we interviewed who specifically said he came to Wilcrest because of its diversity, put it this way:

> We all come together and learn from each other. We also gain a sense of our common creation in the image of God and our common unity in Christ. For me, it's like walking through a garden with many beautiful flowers. I would be impressed to walk through a garden of just red roses, but to walk through a garden with so many beautiful instances of God's creation is far more fascinating to me. It's breathtaking.

An African woman who always comes to worship services in traditional Nigerian dress and head wrap and is held in high esteem for her biblical knowledge told us that at Wilcrest, "We are about serious multi-ethnic business, and that is, at its core, God business." A Mexican immigrant told us, in heavily accented English, that the racial diversity was "holy and Godly. Nations fight each other, but here we no war; we worship, together. It is a God thing, it is God filling us, it is about love." A black woman, who talked about carrying many scars of white racism and who sees the Bible as a story of freeing people from oppression, said of the racial diversity, "It makes Wilcrest a place where my family and I feel included, welcomed, involved. I love to learn from other cultures, and to see how we come together to help each other. We are like a quilt being sewn together."

Many people told us that being part of the racial diversity at Wilcrest had changed them.

> I love to see all the cultures, the different ways of dressing and speaking and communicating. It has changed my view of Christianity. I never thought about how many different cultures and peoples were going to Heaven. I just thought Heaven would look like me and my family. (Cuban American)

> By associating with people in church, worshiping with them, you interact on such a different level. I take that experience into the larger world and I don't have those fears or stereotypes that I once did. That is not to say they are completely erased. But I am better equipped now, to not prejudge people just because of their skin color or their ethnic background. (White)

Although the increased racial diversity has brought much joy and excitement to Wilcrest, it has also brought difficulties for some. In stark contrast to the non-core members of Messiah Fellowship, almost no one at Wilcrest talked about currently feeling left out or having trouble making friends. The feelings communicated by Fernando during his early days of being outside the cliques were rarely mentioned in connection with the present situation. Instead, any difficulties discussed were focused on worship or on cultural misunderstandings.

Most of the non-whites mentioned the desire for at least one of the following: more music from a wider variety of cultures (rather than the white-based hymns and praise music that dominated the music of Wilcrest at the time), longer worship services, more singing, livelier worship, and, important for many, more testimony time. This latter issue—time during worship for people to share publicly about their lives and to testify how God has been working—was often mentioned in the context of something lost, a way for the people of Wilcrest to connect that was not employed nearly enough.

Non-whites and whites alike found that communicating could be difficult. More than one told of struggles communicating across language barriers, or of trying to tell a joke that was not interpreted as such. The issue of time came up often. Particularly Latinos, but also some blacks, talked about struggling to see time as rigidly as whites and Asians in the church see it. "For them, something starting at 10:45 means 10:45 exactly, as if we all could have watches with exactly the same time!" "I am learning how important time is to the whites and Asians in our church. They take it very literally, and very seriously. They seem hurt if I don't come very close to the stated time. I am really having to learn to be 'on time.'"

Some of the whites with whom we spoke communicated hurt, or at least frustration, with different conceptions of time. They thought some people were not taking things seriously enough, and they found this especially frustrating given that the issue at hand was learning about God. One white man, a teacher of an adult Sunday school class, felt his frustration build week after week as people came to his hour-long class fifteen, twenty, even thirty minutes after the scheduled starting time. When he aired his frustration to some of the Latinos, he was told "that if you show up on time all the time, that in their culture that is equated with thinking you are very important and have to be there for things to work. That's not a very Christian trait." So, he mused with some befuddlement, "one culture thinks it offensive not to be on time, the other thinks it offensive to be on time. No easy solution there!"

Some whites, especially those who had been at Wilcrest longer, communicated a sense of losing something, of life at Wilcrest becoming perhaps too different, less familiar, harder to interpret, more complicated. "I miss the old hymns, the great songs of the faith." "I have felt over the last few years that decisions get made and my voice is no longer needed. At a human level, it hurts. I have even thought of leaving. But then I realize I

need to be more mature, more Christian." One white man, David—
known as a deep thinker by others at Wilcrest—reflected on why diversity is perceived to be difficult:

> It challenges the notions of ourselves, who we think we are. And it chal-
> lenges the notions of what we think of other cultures. When we first en-
> counter these things, it gives us a sense that we are losing something.
> The challenge is to convince us that it is worth the risk of losing some-
> thing in our interactions with each other. We are never going to be the
> same once we come to the God understanding that we are truly multi-
> cultural. That is the risk. But it is also the gain.

In conducting the interviews, we heard divergent interpretations of the
support for diversity in membership, worship, or structures of the church.
Whites (except for David) saw the church as extremely supportive of all
things diverse. As one white man said, "our ethnic groups are content.
They are showing that with their presence; they keep coming back." Another white man brought up Fernando as an example of the support
Wilcrest gives:

> We are really trying to integrate a mix into our worship service and our
> programs. The latitude and leeway that the minority lay leaders are
> given in pursuing different avenues to reach folks is excellent. Look at
> Fernando with the way he is allowed to translate the sermon into Span-
> ish. You could look at it as, well, Fernando is translating it into Spanish
> but who is checking Fernando's translation? Who's to say that he's not
> putting in his own slant? The freedom that Fernando has been given to
> do that is but one reflection of our trust and commitment.

These same issues, when discussed by non-whites, sounded different. For
example, while whites saw Spanish translation as something allowed, as
a reflection of trust in, openness to, and support for diversity, non-whites
noted that Fernando had to pursue the idea, present it, and with the help
of the Spanish ministry, raise the thousands of dollars necessary to purchase the equipment. They did this not through an allocation from the
Wilcrest budget, but by holding car washes and Mexican-dinner fund
raisers on their own. Once they had raised the money, the Spanish speakers had to select the equipment to purchase, price it, buy it, set it up, and
staff it completely with volunteers. From this perspective, Wilcrest has

not been particularly supportive. Core members have "allowed" it to occur, but they have not put funds, time, or human power behind their commitment to furthering diversity.

Learning from This Case?

Comparing Wilcrest to Messiah Fellowship is instructive. As at Messiah, members of Wilcrest's core group were much more likely to find their closest friends within their own racial group, when compared to peripheral groups. And as at Messiah, the core group was significantly more likely to have their closest friendships within rather than outside of the congregation.

. Why then did we hear so little talk by the peripheral groups about feeling like outsiders, lacking social attachments, and feeling isolated and excluded, as we did from Messiah's peripheral members? Although we heard reports of such talk occurring earlier in Wilcrest's process of transformation into an interracial congregation, almost no one spoke of such feelings being still present at the time we were conducting our study. We think four factors, when considered together, lead to a different situation than at Messiah Fellowship, and ultimately to a healthier congregation, one more likely to maintain its diversity.

Unlike Messiah Fellowship, the peripheral groups at Wilcrest do not include whites. Whites, we have found over years of study, have less tolerance for not being the core group, the position they are accustomed to in the larger society. Non-whites appear to have greater patience for cultural practices and social structures that do not favor them, in part because these are what they face daily in the larger society. Wilcrest also benefits from a significant contingent of immigrants. Immigrants typically expect to be peripheral, at least for a time. They also expect that they will have to adopt some of the ways of the host society in order to fit in, to succeed economically, to make a new life. Thus Wilcrest has, we think, benefited significantly from the fact that much of its diversity is immigrant based.

Wilcrest has also benefited immeasurably from decisions on the part of a few non-whites that rather than leave, they would dedicate themselves to helping Wilcrest achieve its stated vision (an advantage of having a clear, well-publicized vision statement). It appears to us that in the transformation, there were a few key times when non-whites could have given up, but in part due to the reasons stated above, enough stayed and worked to encourage further non-white growth.

The non-white growth has been key, contributing to the larger absolute size of Wilcrest compared to Messiah Fellowship. There are as many Latinos at Wilcrest as there are people at Messiah Fellowship; the same is true for blacks. This size difference makes for important differences in the experiences of the groups. As one African American woman remarked, "When we first visited Wilcrest, there was only one African American here [Glynn, discussed earlier in the chapter]. And," she told us with a laugh, "my husband said he didn't count as 'diversity' since he is married to a white woman." She and her husband did not stay at Wilcrest at that time, but because they lived nearby, they sent their children to activities at the church, and they would visit periodically. About two years before we were there, they decided to join. She explained the reason to us: "We noticed the change. Now there are so many blacks here, I don't even know them all. I don't know all the Hispanics. My husband said, 'now we are welcomed, this is the place for us.'"

Also according to this woman, Wilcrest benefits much from its trajectory. It is not only the picture that matters; so too does the movie. Wilcrest's multiracial development is not where everyone would like it to be, but people are full of hope, because they see it moving in the direction of becoming more fully interracial. A Mexican American man who expressed that he most appreciated the focus on the Bible and the diversity of people at Wilcrest said, "But I think the diversity could be more. It's going to be more!" This is a general feeling among Wilcrest's members, in large part because that has been their experience.

Since the interviews for this chapter were conducted, a little more than two years prior to this writing, Wilcrest's diversity has increased even further. The congregation now claims representatives from 41 nations (up from 37), and membership has gone from 45 percent non-white to more than 55 percent non-white. Since our interviews, a Korean American has been hired as the children's minister, and an African American has been hired in the newly created position of Associate Pastor of Development (designed to help people incorporate into the congregation and become more involved in its work and mission).

The music has changed as well. The all-white worship band has added a recent Cameroonian immigrant who plays African percussion instruments, such as the congas. With the new ability to play a wider variety of music, the choir director has integrated songs with African and Caribbean flavors. To balance this change, more songs are being sung in Spanish, and more songs from the black gospel tradition are being incorporated as well.

At the time of the interviews, only deacons read Scripture and prayed during services. With one exception, the deacons were all white. Since the interviews, three more non-whites have been ordained as deacons, and several others are in training. And non-deacons now regularly read Scripture and pray during the service. Pastor Woo asked his wife, Sasha, herself the daughter of Mexican immigrants, to be in charge of ensuring that a diversity of people read Scripture. This shift has produced visible changes. A few weeks prior to this writing, a Mexican immigrant woman with a thick accent read the Scripture in English, then in Spanish. She then prayed in both languages, and with much passion thanked God for her Wilcrest family, for the love of the people, and their openness to embrace anyone. "At Wilcrest, Lord, you have given us a place to call home!"

This place that so many people from so many divergent backgrounds call home, a place trying to open its arms to any and all, has a concealed irony. It was Rev. Woo who pointed this out to us: "By our very nature, by our vision, by our appearance, you would think we are open to all groups and all people. But we are not. We are only able to attract and keep people open to worshiping God in the context of multiple groups. People are naturally drawn to people like themselves. By broadening our vision and purpose, we have narrowed the number of people who will enter our doors." Thus, even in what appear to be successfully integrating congregations, larger social forces continue to shape them. But at the same time, as we have seen in glimpses, these congregations are impacting larger social forces.

4

White Flight or Flux?

It is Sunday morning worship service. Pastor Barnes, a middle-aged African American man, asks the Holbert family to join him up front at the pulpit. Bill, Jane, and their three boys walk to the front of the church and join Pastor Barnes. Pastor Barnes asks Jane and Bill to share with the congregation their future plans. Bill approaches the microphone and explains that "God has called our family to walk a different path. While we will miss the congregation, we need to follow God's leading. And sadly," he continues, "following God at this time in our lives requires us to leave Crosstown Community Church." There are a few sighs of sadness from the congregation in response to this news. After Bill finishes, the senior pastor asks the church elders to come up to the pulpit to pray for the Holberts. Pastor Barnes and the elders encircle the family and pray for them asking God's blessing on the family and God's continued guidance. After the prayer, Jane, Bill, and their boys return to their seats in the pews with the rest of the congregation.

Five other families have repeated this scenario at Crosstown Community Church over the past eighteen months. Five of these six families were white and were active members of Crosstown. One family included one of the full-time pastors of the church. For the remaining attendees at Crosstown, this is yet another example of "white flight." Both blacks and whites at Crosstown are concerned that scenes such as these will become more and more common, inevitably leading to a complete racial transition.

In this chapter we examine the process of racial transition in an interracial church, Crosstown Community Church, and the response of church members to the change. We also examine the possible reasons for these changes and consider what might be learned from this case. Crosstown is similar to Wilcrest in that it has a long history of being a predominantly white Baptist church that went through a racial transition as a result of demographic change in the neighborhood. It is also similar to Messiah Fellowship in that whites are a minority at this church, albeit numerically the largest minority group. Crosstown differs, however, from both Messiah and Wilcrest in that African Americans are a majority at this church, both in numbers and in representation in leadership. Another difference is that African American–white racial dynamics are the dominant story here. This black-white dynamic, in the context of neighborhood "white flight," presents key challenges to maintaining the racial diversity at this church.

Crosstown Community Church History

Crosstown is located in Mapleton, an inner-ring suburb that borders the Midwest city of Anderson. The church was founded in 1921 by members of another local church located in Anderson. Historically, Crosstown has been an all white, predominantly middle-class church and an affiliate of the American Baptist Association. At its peak in the 1950s Crosstown had as many as 1,100 members. People came not only from the local neighborhood but from all over the city. The church provided two Sunday worship services to accommodate its attendees. The church was also respected among evangelicals across the metropolitan area for its emphasis on biblical education. Sunday school classes on various biblical topics boasted a weekly attendance that reached well into the hundreds. Longtime members proudly describe Crosstown during its peak as one of the better churches to attend in the metropolitan area.

But Crosstown's attendance slowly dwindled throughout the late seventies and early eighties, until only a small number of members remained. Longtime attenders of the church point to a divide over theological perspectives as the primary cause of this decline. The church had split into two factions[1] over about a five-year period. One of these factions was led by the senior pastor at the time. He and his supporters held strict beliefs on the kinds of cultural practices in which Christians could participate. The legitimacy of a person's Christian identity was questioned if he or she participated in activities deemed ungodly, such as watching certain movies. The senior pastor purported that he should have the final authority on church and religious matters. The other faction believed that the legitimacy of a person's Christianity was not based upon their participation in or abstention from specific cultural practices but on the grace of God. This group felt that church leadership should be more democratic rather than totalitarian.

This divide was very bitter for Crosstown members. Even now, after nearly twenty years, people tell the story with intense emotion, both sadness and anger. As an elderly white woman and member of the "grace" faction recalled this story, she looked her interviewer square in the eyes and with an expression of firm resolve and stubbornness told her "we were not going to let them get away with it."

Ultimately, the "grace" camp prevailed. The senior pastor was eventually removed from office and voted out of the church membership. Those who supported the senior pastor also left. This internal division had so discouraged other regular attenders and members that many had left the church. By the end of the crisis, average worship attendance had decreased to roughly eighty.

The church was in a "weak" and "desperate" state after the crisis. Unable to support a full-time senior pastor financially, it hired a professor from a local Bible college as a part-time interim pastor. With the direction of this pastor, the church began to orient itself toward the local community, which by this time was racially and economically diverse. From accounts of church leaders at the time, there were no objections to this new church vision from the predominantly white membership. The church began to identify as a local community church and opened its doors to its African American neighbors.

In the years since then, attendance at Crosstown has increased. Today, about 200 people attend the weekly Sunday morning worship service. However, the proportion of white attenders has decreased. The greatest decrease has occurred during the current senior pastor's tenure. On average, the adult attendance is about 65 percent African American and 30 percent white. The remaining 5 percent are Asian and Latino. The church leadership, including the pastoral staff, lay leaders, and worship singers, is also racially diverse. Although Crosstown has become increasingly diverse socioeconomically, the church continues to be largely middle-class. Many, regardless of race, hold professional jobs as managers, engineers, and doctors. Furthermore, during the mid 1970s, Crosstown discontinued its membership with the American Baptist Association because the denomination became too theologically liberal for the church. Crosstown remains an independent church today.

The church's interracial status has become central to its identity. This is exemplified in church symbols and literature. The church logo, for example, is a circle of hands of varying skin tones linked together by each hand holding the wrist of the next. Another example is the church's mission statement, which states that the church is "committed to being an inclusive congregation and being intentional in matters of race and class diversity." It further reads that the church aims to "stand courageously at the intersection where race and class collide and daring to live out authentic Christian community."

Mapleton and Anderson

Crosstown's mission, to "stand at the intersection where race and class collide," is not only a statement of action but fact. Crosstown is located on a dividing line between city and suburb, lack and wealth, disadvantage and privilege.

Mapleton is middle- to upper-middle-class. More than 50 percent of the residents of Mapleton have at least a bachelor's degree, and half of these have graduate degrees.[2] The average annual household income is $82,000. Additionally, Mapleton's business district is thriving, with restaurants, professional services, grocery stores, banks, business offices, coffee shops, boutiques, and even a movie theater. The community also hosts festivals, sidewalk sales, and outdoor theater and live music in the parks throughout the year.

Mapleton is a racially diverse suburb—the result of the institutionalization of programs specifically aimed at developing and maintaining racial diversity within the community. Until thirty-five years ago, Mapleton was 99 percent white. Blacks began to move in in small numbers during the 1960s. This trend was soon followed by an exodus of white residents. The neighboring community of Anderson had already begun to experience "white flight." Between 1960 and 1970, the proportion of black residents increased from virtually zero to one-third of Anderson's population (McKenzie 2000). In response to the impending racial changeover, Mapleton's local government passed a housing ordinance—The Neighborhood Stabilization Movement—to stabilize the racial composition of the community. This has included reserving a proportion of the housing stock as rental properties and providing incentives for landlords to rent apartments at affordable rates. By 1972, the seemingly impending "white flight" had tapered off (Goodwin 1979). In 2000, whites and blacks composed 70 percent and 22 percent of Mapleton's population respectively.

The remaining 8 percent include Asians, Latinos, and Native Americans.

In contrast, Anderson is 90 percent African American and is a primarily working-class community. Two-thirds of Anderson residents have graduated from high school. Of these high school graduates, half have at least some college. Although the average annual household income in Anderson is $43,000, the poverty rate is near 20 percent. Moreover, unlike Mapleton, most of the businesses in Anderson are independent fast food restaurants (such as BBQ and soul food spots), dry cleaners, beauty shops, or liquor stores. Many city lots are vacant and overgrown with weeds or serve as resting places for rusting cars or appliances. The neighborhood is also plagued with a pervasive drug culture. According to a community activist in the neighborhood, drugs and gangs are the community's primary problem. During our own observations of the neighborhood, we were aware of the arrests of three teenage black boys and two separate drug. Furthermore, it was not uncommon to see groups of young black men, who appeared to be high-school age or younger, standing on street corners during school hours on weekday mornings and afternoons.

Despite the challenges facing the community, Anderson continues to strive to improve the quality of life in the community. There are at least five local community activist groups in Anderson. Representatives of these groups are negotiating with the city for street improvements, better responsiveness from police and fire departments, and support for attracting national chain businesses. Community gardens have been planted in some of the vacant lots. Programs have been developed to provide adults with entry-level job skills and children with a safe space to play after school. Anti-drug campaigns have also been held to discourage the perpetuation of the drug market in the community.

Crosstown is keenly aware of its "strategic" geographic location. The church currently appeals primarily to the middle and professional classes. However, as demonstrated in the church's mission statement, it desires to further extend its appeal to the working-class and poor residents of Anderson.

Come One Come All

During every Sunday morning worship service, visitors are asked to stand so the congregation can see and greet them. Once the visitors stand, ten or fifteen people from all over the church get up from their seats, walk over to the visitors and personally greet them, often with a smile, a hand-shake, and a "Great to have you!" or "Welcome to Crosstown!" After the visitors have been sufficiently recognized and greeted, everyone is invited to stand and greet other congregants. At this time, those still seated get out of their seats and walk up, down and across aisles shaking hands, giv-ing hugs or pats on the back as they greet their fellow congregants with a "Good morning!" or "How are you doin'?" or "God bless you." If an in-tended "greetee" is too far for a greeter to touch in some way, he or she will wave as they extend their greeting. During this time, one hears all manner of shuffling and laughing. This is one of the loudest times in the service. Most Sundays people return to their seats without coaxing. How-ever, the pastor has at times had to request that people make their way back to their seats.

This weekly ritual illustrates that the friendliness and warmth of Crosstown is an important part of the church's culture. As at Wilcrest, our interviews suggest that this warmth is one of Crosstown's greatest strengths. While our respondents mentioned other draws, such as the ser-mons and the music, the most common response to our question "what do you enjoy most about Crosstown?" was the warmth and friendliness of the church.

Everybody [at Crosstown] was so warm. They made me feel welcome. (African American)

I enjoy the people, the warmth of the community [at Crosstown]. . . . I enjoy the fact that people know my name, know who I am. (Asian)

It's been a good group of folk to know. I'd probably say that's the most exciting thing. (White)

It was just a friendly church. . . . People made you feel welcome. [They] were approachable. (African American)

I think the people are really good [at Crosstown]. I feel they are very friendly and very welcoming. (White)

I enjoy the relationships that I have most of all . . . you know, the friends that we have. (African American)

Although Crosstown attenders feel that the church is a very welcoming, warm place, a majority of respondents reported that their closest friends do not attend the church (see table 4.1). This situation is significantly different from Messiah and Wilcrest; in both of those groups, a majority of people, regardless of race or ethnicity, had their closest friends within the church. Interestingly, even though many Messiah members complained that they were relationally isolated, a much higher percentage of numerical minority members at Messiah had close friendships inside the church than did numerical *majority* members at Crosstown. Yet we did not hear complaints from Crosstown members (neither majority or minority members) about being relationally isolated.

One explanation for this could be that Crosstown members have enough social ties outside of the church that they are not as relationally needy and therefore do not look to the church to meet their needs for friendship. Many of our respondents explained that while they have good friends in the church, they feel closest to those friends whom they have known longer, particularly those whom they have known since they were high-school or college age. Nearly all of these friends are of their same race, as most respondents grew up in racially homogeneous environments.

As at Messiah, the closest church friends of African Americans (the numerical majority) at Crosstown were more likely to be of their same race than were the closest friends of white members (see table 4.2). About three-fourths of African American respondents reported that their closest and second closest church friends at Crosstown were also African American. A slight majority of white respondents reported that their closest church friend was also white. However, 61 percent and 75 percent reported that their second and third closest church friends were of a race other than their own.

While we do see a pattern that majority group members (blacks) at Crosstown are more likely to have close friendships within the church than are minority group members (non-blacks), this difference is not statistically significant. We also see that blacks are more likely than non-blacks to have close same-race friendships within the church. The differences in the mean number of friendships (out of three) being same-race friendships were statistically significant.

So overall, we see majority/minority group differences in friendship networks similar to those found at Wilcrest and Messiah. The interesting difference, however, is the much lower percentage of members at

TABLE 4.1

Analysis of Location of Closest Friends for Crosstown Members
(n = 26)—Inside the Church or Outside the Church?

	Non-Black Members	Black Members
#1 closest friend is inside church	31	40
#2 closest friend is inside church	23	33
#3 closest friend is inside church	30	33
Mean # of 3 closest friends who are inside church	.85	1.07

NOTES: Pearson's Chi-Square test (+ p < .1, * p < .05, ** p < .01)

TABLE 4.2

Percentage of Closest Friends of Crosstown Members
Who Are the Same Race as the Respondent (n = 26)

	Non-Black Members	Black Members
#1 church friend same race	54	73
#2 church friend same race	39	79*
#3 church friend same race	29	54
Mean # of 3 closest friends who are the same race	1.16	2.15*

NOTES: Pearson's Chi-Square test (+ p < .1, * p < .05, ** p < .01)

Crosstown who had their closest friendships within the church, compared to Wilcrest and Messiah.

The Joy of Diversity

Our respondents overwhelmingly reported that they enjoy the racial diversity at Crosstown. Of the sixteen blacks interviewed, eleven reported ethnic diversity as a positive characteristic. Among the ten whites interviewed, racial diversity and the church's friendliness each received nine responses, the greatest agreement reported among the white interviewees for a single item. Both Asians we spoke with reported that the racial diversity of the church was one characteristic that attracted them to it. For most of these interviewees, exposure to an interracial environment has been a rare experience. Many reported that their neighborhood, school, and church were racially homogeneous when they were growing up. Being a part of an interracial church has provided them with opportunities to understand people of another race, to develop cross-racial relationships, and to expand their faith and worldview.

African Americans in particular feel that attending Crosstown has shown them that skin color can be transcended in people's day-to-day experiences. As some African American attenders put it:

I like the diversity because I grew up in a predominantly black church and neighborhood and it has taught me about other races of people. . . . [The diversity at Crosstown] helped me to develop relationships with people outside my race where I felt they were my friend and we share Christ in our life and that they have the same struggles as I do and all of that. . . . I've gotten to know other people on that more personal level where I've said, "wow, you know, it's not that much of a difference."

Others shared similar feelings.

I think it is beneficial to everyone concerned to be exposed to each others' cultures and problems. . . . When you've got all these different people together, they are sharing experiences [and] things in their lives [and] where you [thought] you [were] so different, you find out you're not. You have a lot more in common than you really think. It's just a different color and that's just skin deep, everybody is the same.

I think it's refreshing. It keeps us from falling into stereotypes, you know, that's what I love. It's not the black way, it's not the white way, it's the God way and so I think it's very refreshing. . . . People are able to see past the skin color so I think it's refreshing.

Whites shared that attending an interracial church enhanced their perspective on life or religious experience:

There was something that was missing in my faith growing up in all-white churches when I was little. It just feels like something was missing, I'm not really sure what but it would be very hard for me to go back to an all-white church.

I feel like I get to know more about God as I experience different cultures and different ways of worshiping him.

It really enhances your background and perspective on things. Anytime you get somebody from a different perspective, different upbringing or just a different way of doing things you learn a lot and I really enjoy that.

Crosstown also has at least ten interracial families. The church's diversity provides them with a level of comfort they often do not experience in other contexts. A man in an interracial marriage shared why he enjoyed the diversity at Crosstown:

> No one stared at us. . . . We felt very welcome. We saw other interracial couples. We felt at home. We didn't have to explain anything or like when you go to the grocery store and they ask if [my wife and I] are to-gether—that happens a lot. So we felt welcomed.

For others, being in an interracial environment offers an opportunity to experience the "real world." One African American woman put it this way:

> It's the real world. We live in an ethnic, diverse world. We live in a global world. We've got all kinds of people and I think the church needs to reflect the world that we live in and so I think ethnicity in the church is a good thing.

Living in the "Real World"

The world is indeed a diverse place. However, the "real world" may be the last place Crosstown would want to reflect. As research shows, most of the world is racially segregated in nearly every context in which peo-ple live out their daily lives. This is especially true in the United States, where occupations, neighborhoods, and religious organizations tend to be racially homogeneous (Collins 1995; Tomaskevic-Devey 1993; Fosu 1993; Wilson 1995; Anderson and Shapiro 1996; Massey and Denton 1993; Jackson 1985; Frey and Farley 1996; Emerson and Smith 2000).

Crosstown is an exception. The church has affirmed for many of its members that people can share life and come to understand one another across racial lines. Yet, as more and more whites leave, this utopia is being doubted. Although the people of Crosstown enjoy the rare opportunity of experiencing a racially diverse environment that is also "warm," "friendly," and Christian, they have to reconcile this with what they see as another example of "white flight."

Among the African Americans interviewed, half mentioned that they were concerned about whites leaving the church. Blacks express sadness, frustration, and disappointment about the departure of whites and the potentially lost opportunity to worship in a racially diverse context. For some, it is reminiscent of the neighborhood white flight they and so many other African Americans have experienced in America. One African American woman explains:

> I hope it doesn't go any farther than what it is, where all the white people leave and then the church becomes all black. . . . The neighborhood where I raised my kids was all white. . . . And in about four or five years' time that all changed. Most of the white families had left. . . . So you see . . . it's a common thing and I guess it can happen in the church. I'm starting to see it happen at Crosstown.

Another African American woman shared similar sentiments:

> I'm very sad and frustrated that a lot of the Caucasians are leaving. I didn't want to see that happen. I know it happens when we move in their neighborhoods, they begin to move out. I was just so happy to see blacks and whites praising the Lord together, worshiping together.

Unlike the women quoted above, one African American man was not surprised that Crosstown is following a racial transitioning pattern similar to that seen in other institutions:

> When blacks show up in dominant numbers in the school system whites leave. For whatever reason, these things that prevail outside of the church just carry themselves over into the church and at Crosstown I really don't see it being any different than what I have experienced in the past, whether you are a Christian or non-Christian.

As we saw in the scenario at the beginning of this chapter, whites who have left have not publicly presented racially motivated reasons for leaving. However, African Americans are reluctant to take the explanations offered publicly at face value. They suspect that whites' leaving is motivated at least in part by racial reasons. Here one woman shares the reactions she has heard from other black women about whites leaving the church. Although she tries to refute their positions, she too admits that she believes whites are not being completely honest about their reasons:

Woman: There was a family that went up to the pulpit recently . . . and there was a black lady that was sittin' behind me and she made a comment that was very derogative but she spoke it out in church and she said, "why are they lyin' like this? Why don't they just all get up and leave?" . . . Another lady that I talked to kind of expressed the same thing. She said, "They are liars and they should all get up . . . why don't they just get up [and] leave? Just make this our church?" . . . They said, "They are not being honest. They are sneaking away, couple by couple or family by family." But then I did express to one lady, I said, "Have you ever noticed that some of the black families have left, for different reasons or whatever the reasons might be?" She just responded by saying, "Yeah, but it's not the same thing." So I think there are certain people who feel as though the church is getting ready to make a change and it's gonna become an all-black church.

Interviewer: Do you think there is some truth in what some of these women are saying to you?

Woman: I'm almost inclined to say that I wouldn't have worded it the way they did but I think there might be some deception as to the real reason for their leaving the church. No one wants to get up and say "Oh, I don't want to be here because I know this is getting ready to change to all black" or "I don't want to be a part of this." . . . It would be too crude like. So, I think that yeah, I really do think that there might be some deception as far as them coming out and stating the real reason why [they are] leaving here. . . . I'm prayerful that it's not that, that they are leaving for the reason that they said they are but you can't help but to think there might be something else behind it too.

Another African American woman shares similar feelings. For this woman, the church should be one place where race is irrelevant. Consequently, the departure of whites from the church is particularly disappointing for her.

The more white people I see leave the church, families or couples, the more I'm feeling like, well maybe, you know, what's wrong? Why are they leaving? At one point it seemed to be a very nice . . . whites, blacks, a couple of Hispanic families, some Asian families and singles but now it's beginning to become all African American and it's sad in a sense because I feel as though Christian people have such an obligation to break down racial barriers and such an opportunity and what better way of doing it than praising God, you know, winning more souls and showing people that there are churches in this part of the world who could care less what color you are. But . . . here we go again. The same thing happened in our neighborhood. . . . It's just sad. It gives the impression that they are running as we come in. And I could be wrong, God forgive me.

One African American male with whom we spoke was specifically bothered by the departure of whites who held leadership positions in the church. While he wanted to accept the explanations whites have given for leaving, like the two women above, he has doubts about the truthfulness of these explanations.

I see a lot of the white membership, not a lot, but the ones that are in certain positions leaving, and that bothers me. I try to say well, the explanations that they give for leaving, I understand that. I hear what's being said but sometimes in the back of your mind you think maybe it's some other reason that they might be leaving, I don't know.

There are markedly fewer whites who expressed concerns[3] about the dwindling number of whites in the church. While blacks seem to believe these changes are, at least in part, a result of the increased black presence in the church, the two white respondents who expressed concerns are not suspicious of whites' motives for leaving. They do, however, seem somewhat anxious about the racial changes. One of the white respondents offered this comment:

We seem to be losing some of our white families and I wish we could draw in some more because I don't want to lose our diversity. This week the Johnsons are moving and I don't know what's going to happen with the Martins, if they are going to be moving. Those are two families that we will lose and I'm not sure it will be easy to replace them. It seems to be easier for African Americans to come in than it does for whites to come in for some reason. I don't know why that is. I don't know.

Most of the whites who have left Crosstown have been families with children still in the home, specifically teenagers. This has the second white respondent, a married father of two young boys (three and six years old),[4] particularly concerned. The loss of white families has challenged his commitment to the church. He has begun to wonder if he too will leave as these other families did.

> We've [i.e., he and other church members] talked about the number of Caucasian families with [older] kids who have left. There weren't that many to start with but there have been a few obvious examples and I guess in a way that has bothered me. We're a white family and when our kids get to be in high school will we be dissatisfied enough with the youth program that we'd pull out too? I mean, you think about that sort of thing. . . . I hate to say it but the high school youth group is 99 percent African American and . . . I guess for me, it's not like, oh man, the group should be mostly white but I thought it should definitely approach more [of a] balance at least. I definitely want a presence [of white kids] there but we almost have to be intentional about staying. I don't want that same thing to happen with the young [white] kids that are growing up now and for us to make the same decisions that some of these other white families have already done before us. . . . I've already been kind of thinking [about this] even though that's years ahead for George [his six-year-old son], I'm thinking how can we prevent it?

He goes on to suggest that a possible solution for retaining white families at Crosstown is a collective commitment by whites to stay at the church.

> To be intentional with the other white families I [think] is so important because we [i.e., white attenders] all need to kind of say we need to be committed to this because the tendency is that by the time your [kids] are in high school you start to question are my kids reaching their fullest potential or are they getting fulfillment through the group or are they such a minority they don't have any friends?

This suggestion seems to imply that his commitment to remaining at Crosstown is contingent upon that of other whites, particularly those with children. Moreover, his greatest concern with whites leaving is not that the church is losing its racial diversity, but rather that this decline in diversity will have a negative impact on his children's capacity to make friends, to be fulfilled, and to reach their "fullest potential."

This man is not the only respondent who expressed concerns about the demographic composition of the youth group at Crosstown. Another white respondent, while not concerned about the falling number of whites at the church, expressed similar thoughts. She is also a parent of young children, ages one, two, and five. She spoke about her frustrations and what she'd like to see:

> More clear direction for the youth program. . . . I think the [youth pastor has] done a great job but I think that [he] did such a good job reaching out to the community that the church families weren't necessarily comfortable . . . sending their kids [to youth group] and I don't think I would either. . . . They are harder core kids but you need the church to be a safe haven too. . . . I think we have some really hard kids who have had a really hard life and are just used to dealing with street junk. . . . And you know, we're not there, we're just going to kindergarten next year and we're nervous, you know!

This mother doesn't refer to African American teens specifically, instead choosing to use other words—"community" and "harder core." It can be inferred that she is talking about African American teens since there are few white children in the youth group. Furthermore, although the youth group is predominantly black, the assumption that it is made up mostly of community children is inaccurate. We found from a youth pastor that about 70 percent[5] of the teens who attend the youth group are children of Crosstown attenders. In the past, the youth group was predominantly unchurched youth from Anderson. However, it has been composed of predominantly church kids for nearly ten years.

Despite the young ages of their children, both this mother and the father quoted earlier are already concerned about the racial composition of the current youth group. Both also reported that they have considered leaving Crosstown because of its racial composition.

So . . . Why Are Whites Leaving, Anyway?

There is no one reason why whites have left Crosstown Community Church. Many no longer attend because they have moved out of state to pursue job opportunities or to live closer to extended family. Others have moved to the far suburbs to escape the high housing costs in the city. In-

terviews with two whites who have left Crosstown for these reasons reveal that for them leaving the church was the greatest downside to moving. A man who was in the process of moving to Iowa explained:

> If there were any reason not to move to Iowa it would be because of
> Crosstown. . . . [My wife and I] have found what seems like a good local
> church.

Another former attender, who now lives in a predominantly white suburb, shares similar feelings about leaving the church. She misses the multicultural character of Crosstown and is no longer satisfied with the homogeneity of the people and worship style at mostly white suburban
churches. Although she and her husband have visited a number of
churches since leaving Crosstown more than five years ago, she feels they
have yet to find a church that compares to Crosstown:

> We loved it there. . . . It was an ideal place because you had everything.
> It was a mix of people. . . . People had a lot. People didn't have as much.
> . . . To the mix and style of the service itself. . . . That is one of the things
> that we really miss. . . . You go to a contemporary service, what's called
> a contemporary service out here [i.e., in a predominantly white suburb]
> and you know it's good but it's not the same. It's just not the same.

However, not all reasons for leaving are so benign. For example, two former white attenders of Crosstown told us in interviews that the difficulty
their children experienced acclimating to the largely black youth group
was the primary reason their families left the church, as was suspected by
the concerned father above. One of these former attenders shared the reasons his family left:

> Well one of the primary things was our oldest daughter. . . . I mean she
> stopped coming [to church] a lot of times. . . . Most of my life I looked
> forward to Sunday mornings. And it reached a point now that I just
> wasn't looking forward to Sunday mornings. It was just a great fight to
> get [our daughter] to come. . . . I can recall when she was younger that
> she was like the one white kid amongst a bunch of black girls. . . . And
> in the younger years I felt that they [i.e., black children] sought to in-
> clude her. They really did. But something had happened to her. . . . A
> friend of hers [from the church] really turned tail on her who she [also]

went to school with. . . . So, if anything else I felt that I needed to find a situation in which she felt comfortable.

There were other factors that influenced this interviewee's decision to leave the church, including his dissatisfaction with the sermons, but the comfort of his child was his primary motivation.

Another family also left the church because their teenage son was unable to develop relationships with the other children in the youth group. They specifically searched for an interracial church and felt that Crosstown met their families' needs when they first began to attend. However, as their teenage son became increasingly dissatisfied with the church, the parents decided to find a place where he would be able to "connect" with other youth and continue to grow in his Christian faith. The mother explains:

> By the time he got [to the youth group] he was about the only white kid. They were really reaching out to the Anderson area kids. And so, it was geared for sort of non-Christian kids. . . . And to be honest he felt very out of place. And it wasn't necessarily a black/white issue. It was an inner city/suburban issue. Now that tends to be a black/white issue. . . . And some of Adam's best friends are not of his race. But he was the only one and there were so many inner city kids and his life was so different being a white suburban kid than black inner city kids. There was no one that he was connecting with as far as friendships go. . . . And so we really had to take into consideration his needs and felt like if we wanted to keep him growing spiritually we had to do something for him. So we began to look and found a place where he was much more happy.

This parent shares similar ideas about the composition of the youth group, as did the young mother above. She also contends that the youth group was composed mainly of non-Christian, inner-city children. As a result, she and the son felt that his spiritual needs were not being met. Moreover, despite her son's capacity to develop interracial friendships in other contexts, he was unable to develop interracial friendships with the other teens in the youth group. This she attributes to the socioeconomic background of the teens in the youth group. Hence, the race and supposed class and lack of religious commitment of other teens in the youth group contributed to her son's inability to develop friendships and increase his faith in the Crosstown youth group.

Black parents also share concerns about the youth group. However, these concerns have much less to do with its composition; instead they focus on the dress code and the kinds of conduct allowed by youth pastors. One black mother told us:

> I just felt that [the youth pastors] were somewhat lax, where the boys would come in with caps on and bandanas and the baggy pants and it's kind of hard to tell your son that it's unacceptable in church . . . when the other kids [who] come in were dressing the same way. . . . I just think that there needs to be a standard set, you know, when the youth are interacting because they need to understand that God's house is a place of worship.

She finally stopped requiring her sons to attend the youth group because of the relaxed dress code.

Another former white attender of Crosstown left for reasons that did not involve his children. His children were satisfied with the youth group. He, however, wanted to be more actively involved in the church and felt that he was being excluded from participating in church activities outside of worship service attendance. He had made multiple attempts to participate in more of a leadership capacity in the church, but these attempts were, according to him, hindered by the pastor and elders. This, he believes, is in part because the pastor was not fond of him for reasons he does not fully understand. He shares a story about one of the instances where he brought his concerns to church leadership:

> I questioned Pastor Barnes about why [I was] being sidetracked. And [he responded to me], "Do you want to do Sunday school class?" So, I didn't know. Was I being insulted or was the Sunday school department being insulted? Is it [that] somebody who is out of [the pastor's] favor is allowed to do Sunday school class or "Sunday school class is really insignificant so let's just give that to Mike." So I felt a double insult there.

The offer to teach Sunday school implied to this former attender that he was being excluded from full church participation. Hence, to some extent, this respondent's angst with the church had more to do with his inability to attain a leadership position. He goes on:

> All week long [people at work] thank me. Everybody is so happy with the work I do. I get affirmation from family. I get affirmation in every-

thing I do. I get affirmed. But then I go to church and I come home just totally empty and frustrated.

Consequently, this feeling of exclusion was rather foreign to him, and it contributed to his dis-ease with the church.

White Flight or Flux?

With a certain sense of resignation, Ms. Ella Stales, an African American member of Crosstown Community Church, says: "We got along. I didn't have any problems. I just looked up one day, and they were all gone." "They" are the whites who lived on her block when she first moved to a predominantly white neighborhood in the early seventies. The neighborhood is Anderson.

Ms. Stales's account is an illustration of how blacks experience neighborhood white flight. She experienced no struggle or outward animosity from her white neighbors. They were friendly and, at least from her perspective, she and her neighbors "got along." However, despite her apparently good relations with them, over time, they moved out one by one until one day there were hardly any whites left on her block. Her experience is in some ways analogous to that of African Americans at Crosstown. According to most accounts, Crosstown is a warm, friendly, welcoming church. People get along well across racial lines. Many of Crosstown attenders' close friendships at the church are interracial relationships. Nevertheless, whites are leaving the church.

African Americans at Crosstown try to be understanding and supportive of white attenders who decide to leave. Yet they cannot help but wonder if the reason whites are leaving is at least in part racially motivated. More specifically, they suspect whites are leaving because of blacks' increased presence in the church. Their experiences with the mass exodus of whites in other contexts have informed this perspective. Moreover, the departure of whites is especially disheartening given these African Americans' presumption that the church is one place where skin color should not matter.

To a certain extent, their suspicions are warranted. Four whites we interviewed, including both current and former attenders, expressed concerns about the largely black youth group. Both of the former attenders explained that their teenage children were unable to identify with their black peers and found it difficult to develop relationships with the black teens in the group. The responses of current attenders are particularly revealing. These white parents of very young children are already contemplating the effect attending a largely black youth group would have on their children. Despite the lack of actual evidence, they believe that the youth group, with the "harder core," "community" kids, is not a safe place for their children. Furthermore, they suggest that their children may not be able to meet their "fullest potential" attending a predominantly black youth group. These perspectives were not limited to Crosstown parents. Similar sentiments were voiced by white parents about the children and youth in the mostly Latino and Black youth group at Wilcrest and the mostly Asian children's group at Messiah.

Concerns about the youth group are echoed by some of the black parents. However, the complaints of black parents have more to do with the rules and expectations the white youth pastors set for the youth than with the race or background of the youth. Moreover, to our knowledge, African Americans have not left or considered leaving the church because of their concerns about Crosstown's youth group.

We must also consider the racial composition of the local community when analyzing the reasons for racial transitioning at Crosstown. Approximately 70 percent of Crosstown's attenders live in Mapleton or Anderson. With the exception of a few families, the remaining attenders live in other nearby suburbs and neighborhoods. Anderson is 90 percent African American and 5 percent white. Mapleton is 22 percent African American and 70 percent white. The racial composition of the neighborhoods combined is 69 percent African American, 25 percent white, and 6 percent Asian, Latino, and Native American. Crosstown has intentionally changed its geographic orientation toward the surrounding neighborhoods. The church is decidedly a neighborhood church, rather than a commuter church. Its racial composition is therefore linked to that of the local community. When we consider this situation, Crosstown, which is about 65 percent African American and 30 percent white, is almost a racial cross-section of its surrounding communities. In fact, whites attend Crosstown in numbers slightly disproportionate to those for the wider community.

Additionally, although there is apparently a decrease in the proportion of white members at Crosstown, there are still whites who have recently begun attending the church, and there are black families who are leaving. The church's record of new regular attenders over the past two years reveals that about 25 percent of newcomers are white and about 10 percent are Asian or Latino. Church records also show twelve African American families who no longer regularly attend Crosstown. Many of these families were not involved in visible church activities (i.e., lay leadership, worship team, or announcements), likely making their absence less noticeable.

Overall, however, there is evidence of white flight taking place at Crosstown. Whites have left the church for racially motivated reasons, specifically the dominant presence of African American teens in the youth group. However, the jury is still out, so to speak, on whether the white flight will lead to a complete racial succession. The church may merely be in a state of white flux or demographic change in the type of whites who attend. For example, among the recent regular attenders who are white, none have teenage children and more than one third are members of interracial families. The continued introduction of new white attenders into the congregation suggests that the church will not experience a complete racial turnover. Moreover, it is difficult to assess whether the racial transitioning occurring at Crosstown is largely the result of non-racial factors or factors external to the church, or largely a phenomenon of whites (particularly parents with teenagers) fleeing blacks.

Learning from This Case

There are four key lessons that can be learned from the case of Crosstown Community Church. First, many attenders of Crosstown, both former and current, desire to worship at an interracial church. Some respondents specifically chose Crosstown for this reason. Interestingly, the group of respondents who chose Crosstown because it is interracial included a disproportionately high number of whites. Second, most of our interviewees at Crosstown, regardless of race, experience the church as a warm, welcoming, and friendly place. Although most respondents reported that their closest friends are of their race, many have close interracial friendships with fellow churchgoers. Former attenders of Crosstown also reported having close friendships with people when they attended Crosstown, many with someone of another race. Some former attenders have even maintained these relationships with Crosstown members after leaving the church. Third, whites are leaving the church in numbers disproportionate to their representation in the congregation. Although some are being replaced by other whites, the retention of whites poses a challenge to Crosstown. Fourth, the departure of whites has a greater impact on African Americans than on whites, and it undermines congregants' faith in the possibility of interracial social contexts. Eight of the sixteen African Americans we interviewed were concerned about the loss of whites at Crosstown, compared to two out of eleven whites. Not surprisingly, their concerns stem from their experiences with racial transitioning in other contexts. Moreover, the decline of white presence in the church is particularly disappointing because African American members trusted that Christian whites would be more accepting of racial integration with blacks. Although they are somewhat reluctant to do so, they attribute the departure of whites to whites' discomfort with the increased number of blacks in the church.

This case, therefore, has a number of similarities to Wilcrest and Messiah, and a number of differences. As at Messiah, whites are in the minority at Crosstown and are less likely to have their closest friendships within the church than are those in the majority group. However, friendships and relational isolation seem not to be a pressing issue at this church because most members appear to have sufficient friendships outside the church, taking pressure off of the congregation to provide those ties. As at Wilcrest, a number of whites have left as a result of the increased presence of other ethnic groups. This trend seems to be creating more resentment at Crosstown, however, as many African Americans in this congregation have experienced white flight in their neighborhoods and are discouraged by their perception that a common faith in Christ was not enough to keep white members from fleeing.

5

Embrace and Division

9:30 a.m.

As I enter the sanctuary of Brookside Community Church in suburban Los Angeles, sounds of a traditional hymn played on an organ fill the air. A friendly middle-aged white man greets me with an outstretched hand and a warm smile. The pews are filled mostly with middle-aged white people, quiet and focused on the front of the church. The service begins with a prayer, and a guitar player leads the worship band, which includes a keyboard player, drummer, flute player, and backup vocalists. All but the keyboard player are white. The congregation stands and sings heartfelt choruses shown on the large video screens up above the pulpit. The "worship time" ends with the congregation belting out the choruses of "How Great Thou Art," a favorite Protestant hymn of the twentieth century. A few announcements are read, followed by a prayer and the beginning of this week's sermon by Mike Van Egan, the head pastor of Brookside. The congregation is attentive and focused on the words of the preacher as he delivers a clear, coherent message on the responsibility of Christians to love people around them who are different.

11:00 a.m.

The experience of entering the sanctuary at this time is remarkably different. An African American man greets me warmly and hands me a program. Church members laugh and hug each other as they enter the sanctuary. At the front of the sanctuary, a racially mixed gospel-style choir is swaying back and forth to the smooth tones of the music, as people in the pews lift their hands and move to the beat. Some are visibly moved by the singing and have tears in their eyes. A middle-aged black man and a middle-aged white man hold their hands together above their bowed heads in a show of spiritual unity. The sanctuary is now filled with a diverse group that includes Latinos, African Americans, and whites of all ages, from small children to elderly men and women. As the song ends in a rousing crescendo, the congregation claps and the keyboard player shouts praises to God. The words to the next song are in Spanish, but the upbeat tones are decidedly African American gospel. Following the final song, an African American man leads the congregation in prayer for several minutes. His voice rises and falls as he invites God to visit the congregation this morning. The congregation responds with clapping and with affirming statements of "yes Lord" and "Amen." Preceding the sermon this time, a Latino man gives announcements and a Latino woman reads today's Bible verse in Spanish. Mike Van Egan then delivers the same sermon that he delivered at 9:30, but he seems a little more animated and expressive.

Following the service, Mike and one of the other white pastors at Brookside stand toward the back of the church and warmly greet members as they file out of the church, grabbing hands and giving hugs. Others stick around and laugh with each other. These two church services at Brookside are so strikingly different that they seem like two different churches.

A History of Ethnic Transformations

The history of Brookside is the story of a church continually striving to adapt to a community undergoing successive ethnic transformations throughout the twentieth century. This suburb of Los Angeles began as a predominantly Dutch community in the early part of the century, a community which at that time was on the edge of urban development. During the postwar expansion of suburbs in southern California, housing tracts emerged and the population became less Dutch and more assimilated Euro-American. During the 1970s the Latino and black populations grew, and white flight to more distant suburbs began; this exodus accelerated in the 1980s. Over time, the suburb was transformed from a middle-class white enclave to a working- and lower-class Hispanic and black community. According to Mike Van Egan, the Rand Corporation, which conducted a study of U.S. cities in 1982, declared this suburb an "urban disaster area" and placed it among the ten worst cities in the nation in terms of urban decay.

Since then, the suburb has stabilized, but it remains decidedly working- and lower-class. It has also become more and more Latino: its census 2000 population was 72 percent Latino, 13 percent black, and 9 percent white.

Brookside has struggled to adapt and remake itself in response to these ethnic transformations in its community. It began in 1925 as a predominantly Dutch-speaking congregation. At the height of its Dutch era, the congregation had more than 500 members, almost all of them first-generation Dutch immigrants. During the postwar transformation from a Dutch to a Euro-American community, the church began to lose members; the Americanized children of the original Dutch members and the Euro-American members of the community were not drawn to the culturally Dutch aspects of the congregation. By 1970, the head pastor had left, and only 200 older members remained; the leaders of the church began to wonder whether it might be wise to close the doors and move on.

Instead of shutting down, the church hired a new pastor—Mike Van Egan's father, Brent. Brent, a Dutch pastor in the Midwest, did not want to work in another Dutch congregation, but according to Brent, God had other plans. The way Brent tells it, he rejected the offer to come to Brookside, but then felt physically sick every time his body faced any direction but west—toward California. When he faced west, his stomach felt fine and he felt a sense of peace. He claims that he took the job at Brookside only to avoid throwing up.

When Brent came to this dying Dutch congregation, he proclaimed that this was going to be a "community church" that would stay in this community and minister to whoever the neighbors were. Brent vowed that he would die ministering in this community. From 1970 to 1990, under the leadership of Brent Van Egan and his son Mike, the church was transformed from a dying Dutch congregation to a thriving Euro-American congregation. English was used exclusively and the church reached out to the Euro-American population in the neighborhood. As a result, the church became culturally more Euro-American. Unfortunately for the church, this period of transformation to a culturally Euro-American church coincided with the transformation of the community to predominantly black and Latino.

By the early 1990s, the church had grown to more than a thousand members, almost all of them white. However, very few of these members

lived in the community—most drove in from surrounding all-white suburbs. In 1993, the elders of the church began to discuss the idea of moving the church to an adjacent all-white suburb to better serve its con-
stituents. Many felt that the church, if it stayed in its current location,
would eventually die out. Brent and Mike Van Egan argued otherwise.
They reiterated Brent's proclamation of twenty years earlier—this is a
community church that will stay in this community and love whoever its
neighbors are. Mike Van Egan now repeats his father's vow—that he too
will die in this community, ministering to its people.

The realization that the church would eventually die if it remained a
white church, however, prompted Mike, who in the early 1990s took over
the head pastor position, to try to steer the congregation through yet another cultural transformation. He reasoned that Brookside had to change
if it wanted to reach its Latino and black neighbors. But he realized that
a church of 1,000 white members, with an all-white leadership, would
not be able to attract a multiracial constituency. According to Mike, "if
you're black and you walk into this all-white church, you may like the
people there and you may think the sermon was wonderful, but you're
going to say—'this isn't for me—I don't fit.'"

The leadership of the church, with Mike as the main force, started the
11 o'clock service as an attempt to create an environment where people
of all ethnic backgrounds could feel like they fit in. Central to Mike's plan
was to extract the few non-white members of the church, develop them
as leaders, and make them a key part of leading and directing the new 11
o'clock service. He calls this "cheating" or "sneaking" their way into creating a multiethnic congregation where none existed before. Twenty-five
non-white members of the church and twenty-five white members went
through a leadership training program Mike organized, and committed
to starting and leading the 11 o'clock service for three years.

As this leadership team of fifty members began planning and strategiz-
ing about how to make the service more attractive to the surrounding
community, other volunteers from the church made 25,000 phone calls to
homes in the surrounding community. Callers stated that they were a
church that wanted to start a multiethnic service where all kinds of people would feel welcome and could worship together. Two thousand people responded positively to this statement and were called again and invited to the inaugural 11 o'clock service in 1997. Three hundred fifty people, mostly black and Latino, came to this inaugural service. Mike and
several other leaders wept as they looked out at the pews filled with black

and brown faces. Their dream of having a service filled with members of the surrounding community was realized.

Within a month of that inaugural service 150 people were regularly attending the 11 o'clock service. About a third of these attenders were white church members who wanted to be involved in the multiethnic service; the remaining two-thirds were new recruits from the surrounding community. Currently, there are 300 regular attenders at 11 o'clock. Approximately one-third are white, more than half are Latino, and the rest are African American. The two earlier services (at 8 o'clock and 9:30), which together serve approximately 1,000 regular attenders, are still overwhelmingly (88 percent) white.

Integration Orchestrated from Above

The leadership of Brookside will tell you that only through God's power could a white middle-class church draw black and brown people into its congregation. This may be true, but the racial integration of the 11 o'-clock service is also a result of very conscious planning by the leadership of the church. Mike hired a talented African American musician to lead the music worship for the service. The music is upbeat and often combines gospel and salsa rhythms to produce a more lively and expressive worship experience than exists in the predominantly white services. Singing is led by a racially mixed gospel choir. Some songs are in English and some in Spanish, with their words projected onto large video screens for all to read. Spanish speakers wear wireless headphones that translate the sermon into Spanish. Bible verses are read by members of the congregation in English and Spanish. Greeters at the door and people leading prayer up front during the service are of all ethnicities. Mike states that "we have a heart to be multiethnic, and you have to show that heart by who you have leading the service."

Mike has also asked a significant core of white members of Brookside to commit to the 11 o'clock service for three years. He has found that most white members of the congregation prefer to stay with the predominantly white services, so in order to keep a white presence in the 11 o'-clock service, he needs to ask people to make a commitment to it. Some of these white members have stayed with the 11 o'clock service after their three-year commitment ended, but many have returned to the other services. As a result, Mike continually asks other white members to commit to the service for a set time in order to replace those white members who have returned to the predominantly white services.

In addition to hiring an African American music leader, Mike recently hired a full-time African American pastor and a full-time Latino pastor for the 11 o'clock service. Thus, preaching at the 11 o'clock service rotates between the white pastors on staff (Mike, Brent, and Mark Richards, the college pastor), Rod Jenkins (the African American pastor), and Luis Arreguin (the Latino pastor). The 11 o'clock service is racially integrated at every level, from the pews to the pulpit.

A final key element of Brookside's success in attracting members of the surrounding community to the 11 o'clock service is their aggressive community outreach and service. The church has a food ministry where needy members of the community can buy food at vastly reduced prices, an after-school tutoring ministry for children, a sports program for youth, and a medical and dental clinic for low-income members of the community. These services draw members of the community into contact with the church by offering an opportunity for them to have specific needs met. The leaders of these ministries can then invite participants in these programs to church services and events.

Feeling Love and Acceptance

In our interviews with attenders of Brookside's 11 o'clock service, many reported that the most powerful draw for them at the service was the atmosphere of love and acceptance. These statements were much like those given by Crosstown and Wilcrest members. Many expressed that they had never seen a place where such a diverse group of people could be so loving to each other.

> There is a nice mixture of people—Latino, black, Caucasian—everyone is so lovable. Everyone likes everyone. They have no fronts with nationalities. . . . It's so cool, [the diversity] is the best part. It is all comfortable for the nationalities. . . . Hispanic, white, black. They're all a family. They meet you and call you brother and sister and hug you. I really like it. I have never been to a church with so much love. (African American)

At the eleven service there are all types of people. I hate racism and coming here there are all types of people, loving and accepting one another
(mixed race).

In particular, the pastors' love of the parishioners was expressed repeatedly.

They honestly are great pastors . . . so real and honest and they love us.
Mike makes me feel comfortable. The first time I came to church, he saw
me in the back and I could see him tear up. After the service, he came to
the back and prayed for me. He always makes me feel welcome. Without a father growing up, I missed the hugs and stuff. Even though he's a
man too, I feel like he is my father at church. I never had a father hug
me, so it feels good when he does. (Mixed race)

Everyone is really comfortable and feels at home. I honestly think that
the pastors would give you what ever you needed. I can't imagine all the
time it takes to run all of this, yet they still have time for us. (White)

The words "comfortable" and "accepted" often came up in our interviews. Many non-white respondents told us that the diversity of the
church made them feel more comfortable. A number of people expressed
that they had visited all-white churches and hadn't felt welcomed or accepted. Others who came from mixed-race backgrounds or were in mixed
marriages experienced the diverse environment as one of the few places
where they didn't feel as if they stood out. For those who have grown up
and live in diverse environments, a diverse church seems to feel more welcoming and comfortable than a racially homogeneous environment.

It is good all the blacks and Mexicans, and the people from everywhere.
I don't know if it helps the church but it helps the people to know there
is no racism in their church. It makes me feel good and accepted. (Hispanic)

The high school I went to was diverse, so I have been around other races
and cultures. The church I grew up in was all white. It's neat to see us all
together and doing the same things though we have different backgrounds. I have a friend who comes whose husband is Puerto Rican.
He's happy here. He likes being in a place where he isn't the only non-

white person. With the activities the church has, the people in the community see there are more races and backgrounds at the church. They are more likely to join. (White)

Because it is multicultural it's more comfortable. It doesn't matter what race you are or what your past is. They are much more traditional at the earlier service and more free at the eleven service. I just feel more open and comfortable at the 11 o'clock service. . . . When you look around and you see the different faces and you feel like you fit in, it's like you're not the only one. When I was younger that's how I felt, like I was an oddball. (Mixed race)

This sense of feeling at home and being accepted seemed to be particularly salient for the Hispanic members we interviewed. A number of them reported going to white churches and feeling that they were not accepted by white members. The feeling of acceptance and being at "home" that seems to have come with racial diversity is significant; it seems to be a main draw for non-whites and interracially married couples at all of the other churches we studied.

Friendships within the Church

In contrast to some of the other organizations we studied, most notably Wilcrest and Messiah, there was not a large difference at Brookside between the numerical minority groups and the majority group in terms of their relational connectedness. This is probably due to the unique structure of the organization. Concentrating most of the minority group members into one service, where they are actually the majority, seems to have ameliorated the problem of finding belonging in a majority-dominated organization.[1]

However, some interesting differences between racial groups did emerge. Whites were more likely to have same-race friendships than non-white groups at Brookside's 11 o'clock service (table 5.1). On average, two out of the three best friends (within the church) of white members were of their same race, while only one in three best friends of non-white members were their own race. However, non-white members appear slightly more likely than whites to have their closest friends within the church. On average, 1.7 out of the three best friends of non-white mem-

TABLE 5.1

Percentage of Brookside Members' Closest Friends within the Church Who Are the Same Race as the Respondent (n = 24)

	Non-White Members	White Members
#1 church friend same race	53	67
#2 church friend same race	24	67*
#3 church friend same race	35	67
Mean # of 3 closest friends who are the same race	1.12	2.00

NOTES: Pearson's Chi-Square test (+ p < .1, * p < .05, ** p < .01)

TABLE 5.2

Analysis of Location of Closest Friends for Brookside Members (n = 26)—Inside the Church or Outside the Church?

	Non-White Members	White Members
#1 closest friend is inside church	44	50
#2 closest friend is inside church	69	17*
# 3 closest friend is inside church	64	50
Mean # of 3 closest friends who are inside church	1.71	1.17

NOTES: Pearson's Chi-Square test (+ p < .1, * p < .05, ** p < .01)

bers were within the church, as contrasted with 1.2 out of three best friends for white members (table 5.2).

The higher likelihood of same-race friendships among white members, despite their status as numerical minorities in the 11 o'clock service, is probably related to the fact that whites have opportunities to interact with other whites outside of the context of that service (Bible studies, outreach ministries, etc.), groups where they are in the majority. It is more difficult to explain the higher likelihood of non-white members having their closest friendships within the church. One possible explanation is that white members are more likely to be commuters from other neighborhoods, where they may have their primary friendship ties in their own predominantly white communities, while non-white members are from the surrounding community. The difference between white and non-white, however, is small and not close to being statistically significant.

Overall, differences between majority and minority in their ability to form friendships were smaller in this church than at any of the other churches we studied. We suspect that this reflects the "church within a church" structure of the organization. Whites, being the minority at the 11 o'clock service, have many opportunities to connect to other whites at other church functions. Non-whites, being the minority in the church as a whole, are concentrated in the 11 o' clock service, where they have many opportunities to connect to people who have similar backgrounds. Also, there are sufficient absolute numbers of the main racial groups (black, white, Hispanic) that members of each of these groups have opportunities to interact with those who are culturally similar.

The Benefits of Multi-ethnic Worship

Our interviews also showed that the diverse nature of the service was the primary attraction for many people. As we have seen in the other case studies, worshiping around people who are culturally different seems to be spiritually enriching for many participants.

> The multi-ethnic church makes me understand more about people that I have met and people from other places. I see their faces and understand their backgrounds and I think it is very interesting. It helps to understand the others' lives and how they talk to God. I like understanding their backgrounds and personalities. (Hispanic female)

In particular, a number of people stated that people from other backgrounds help them to understand God in a different way, and give them a greater sense of freedom to express themselves.

> I think people of color that are in the church help to bring a looser interpretation of the Dutch reformed stance. A lot of people of color come from Pentecostal backgrounds, lots of my friends have commented and say "how can those earlier service people just sit there and do nothing?" They bring freedom to express oneself. With each passing month it seems that we learn more and more. I have a friend who came and saw the inspirational choir, she just started jumping, dancing, hooting and hollering. I knew that there were people who would have scolded her for that [at the earlier services]. They hadn't been that open before. It's hard to sit there and not do anything. The various ethnicities are helping us be freer to express ourselves. (White)

It's nice to have such diversity [among the pastors] too. They each have such different styles and ways of speaking. It totally adds flavor. Each has different outlooks on things. (White)

Every group brings something to the group, everyone contributes something. Not better or worse, it's just different. Every group's participation contributes to and enhances the service. One way is not good, but there are other foods to taste too. It really helps the young people experience and praise with others. It's a wealth of richness of social and ethnic backgrounds. It's good for the kids to learn it then go out in the world. We older people have hang-ups, but we can really teach our kids through this. (African American)

In addition to the spiritual benefits, a number of people reflected that they had changed their views of other ethnicities by worshiping with them.

It's really about getting to know people and growing to dissolve the stereotypes you have of people. You get to know people and you realize that they aren't the way you thought they would be. When I was growing up, my father would always talk bad about the black people that were in our neighborhood, or that we saw. He had such bad stereotypes and he wouldn't allow us to associate with black people. It's different now though. He sees our lives and our commitment to this church, he respects it. He understands now that we all need to learn from each other and understand other people. My kids go here and have friends that are of all different races. It's good for them, I never got to have that. It's important to understand all types of people, it helps us to live better in this world. (Hispanic)

Overall, most respondents cited the diversity of the service as the main reason they chose to come to Brookside, and as one of the things they like the most about attending there. Particularly interesting in this church is the recurring statement that the diversity of the church made them feel more comfortable and accepted. The leaders of this service seem to have created an atmosphere of warmth of love that is contagious, leading to a sense of home and belonging for most people involved.

The Challenge of Language

The primary challenge to the smooth integration of different ethnic groups into the 11 o'clock service at Brookside seems to be the issue of language. As was mentioned before, the service provides translation through headphones to people who are primarily Spanish speakers. One or two songs during the service are also sung in Spanish, and the Bible is read in both English and Spanish. For some, this combination of languages adds to the spiritual richness of the service.

> I like to hear all the different languages' prayers. I don't have a problem having Spanish subtitles, it's awesome to have their native language. It really works out for the good. (Mixed race)

> I like the worship and the songs in Spanish and English, and when they throw in some soul, too. They try to incorporate more hallelujahs and more of the amens. It's nice to see all the different colors and shades. The worship is really designed for everyone. (White)

> I think it's great. Because it's not all one group of ethnicity and because there is an opportunity for us to sing songs in Spanish. We read scripture in Spanish and pray in Spanish. It's a large part of the diversity, it meets the needs of the group. It makes them feel good and comfortable by breaking down barriers. We had soul Sunday and used the African American ideas of praise and worship. On Cinco de Mayo, the whole service will be in Spanish. It's an opportunity for different things and openness. We get to try new things. (African American)

In contrast to some members' enthusiasm for a multilingual service, others found the combination of languages distracting and disorienting. Some felt that the translation created segregation in the service.

> I really don't enjoy listening to the services in both English and Spanish. It's hard for me to sit through that. I like the ear [phones] for those people. But they listen to them too loud and then I can hear everything they say. They usually sit there all together and you just know not to sit there with them. I am afraid they would feel put off, or that we don't like

them . . . really, it's just all the noise that we don't like. They don't realize how loud they are talking sometimes. (White)

I feel a little uncomfortable with the 11 o'clock service if they do too much translation of English into Spanish. I don't speak much Spanish. I feel uncomfortable, even though they say it in English too. I think I am impatient. Especially when they do the whole service, I just don't enjoy it as much. (Filipina)

A number of Hispanics we interviewed felt that other members disliked the Spanish parts of the service.

Sometimes I feel that they put to much emphasis on being Hispanic. . . . It throws the English-speaking people off. I have heard comments that when some people come to the 11 o'clock service, they are uncomfortable with the Spanish. The balance is really hard. One lady wants more contemporary music in the service, but she didn't like the Spanish. (Hispanic)

Hispanic member: Well, there are some people, Spanish-speaking people, that love the Spanish in the church because they don't speak any English. They want to use the earphone translations. I know it sounds a little loud. I will ask them to turn it down sometimes. I know that people won't sit by the Hispanic people because of that noise.
Interviewer: Do you think that can create a barrier between people at the service?
Hispanic member: I think so. There are people that you can tell right away. They love the 11 o'clock service, but they don't want to see us there.
Interviewer: Why? How do you know that?
Hispanic member: I can tell by the feelings that they show me. Sometimes I can see their attitudes. Probably they don't want the translations. They want Spanish-speaking people to understand more English. There are a lot of people who just don't know English.

In addition to this feeling that others are irritated by the Spanish portions of the service and the translations, a number of Hispanics we interviewed felt that Spanish-speaking people could not fully participate in church activities and were left out of leadership because of the language barrier.

Some who speak both Spanish and English say that others assume that they are Spanish-only speakers and therefore would not be able to perform certain tasks.

> I am bilingual but they don't involve me. They have some women's Bible studies, but I always feel awkward when I go. They really should try to get some other non-English-speaking women to get involved. They don't even ask us to cook for activities. Women in the Spanish Bible study have more potential that they don't tap into. Spanish-speaking people also can't get involved in [outreach ministry] because there is no translation. If it wasn't for my translation of the [outreach] service to my husband, he wouldn't have become a Christian. They just never use us. We are so segregated, we are always separated into our segregated groups. (Hispanic)

The leadership of the church has thought about this issue and understands the difficulty of fully integrating speakers of different languages into a single church. It is one thing to allow Spanish speakers to enjoy a song or two in their language and to hear the sermon in Spanish, but quite another to integrate them fully into the leadership and social life of the church. After much debate, church leaders have decided to create a Spanish-only service and a number of Spanish-only groups and ministries. Mike and the leadership recognized that some of the Spanish-speaking members could only be full participants in church activities and in leadership in a Spanish-only environment.

This decision, however, has saddened Mike and the other pastors because they know that by creating Spanish-only services and ministries, they will divide the 11 o'clock service by drawing out the Spanish speakers into a different set of organized activities. People who formerly worshiped together on Sunday will no longer see each other within the same worship environment. They recognize that while this decision will give Spanish speakers a greater opportunity to participate in the life of the church, it will come at the cost of making the 11 o'clock service less diverse.

Different Services or a Divided Church?

Apart from the challenges presented by language, the 11 o'clock service at Brookside seems to function surprisingly well despite its diverse population. Much of this success seems to come from of its emphasis on diverse leadership and on love and acceptance. Many regular attenders of the 11 o'clock service, however, reported that they do not feel the same acceptance from members of the earlier, predominantly white services. All of the church activities and ministries, other than the Sunday services, combine members from all three services. Many black and Hispanic respondents reported when they came into contact with white members of the other services they felt those white people rejected and looked down upon them. This was by far the most frequently mentioned problem among black and Hispanic respondents. Economic class differences between the predominantly white middle-class members and the working- and lower-class Hispanics and blacks seem to be involved in this perception of rejection.

> Mixed-race member: I feel a lot of uneasiness at the 9:30 service. I don't know a specific reason, but I always felt inferior. There is more like family and community at the 11:00 service.
> Interviewer: Do you feel inferior, or uncomfortable because it's not your style?
> Mixed-race member: It's an overall impression that I can't pinpoint. My husband went to the [private school sponsored by Brookside] and there is just a different atmosphere. The private school kids verses the public school kids. The private school kids get the cars right when they get their license . . . it's just the economic aspect really. You can see the woman with all the makeup and jewelry. There is an arrogance with the way they dress and approach you. 11 o'clock service woman are as beautiful . . . they are more about the inward beauty.

A number of respondents complained that when they go to activities where people from all of the services are combined, they don't feel accepted.

> Hispanic member: Mike will say things in the service like "my brown brothers and sisters." I think the people who attend the earlier services should hear him say that because I don't think they see us like that. I feel that I have accepted them, but they haven't accepted me.
> Interviewer: What did you mean when you said that I have accepted them but they haven't accepted me?

Hispanic member: For example, at the Easter celebration, I was at a table and I was the host. A woman didn't even know that I went to the church. They thought I was a guest. I was dressed the same way she was though. I really felt like I was in my home, but they didn't even know that this was my church. One of my friends won't go to the earlier services because she doesn't have nice clothes.

This type of statement was common among black and Hispanic respondents:

Interviewer: Do you think that you fit in with the people from the other services?
African American member: No, not at all.
Interviewer: Why?
African American member: It might sound weird. As much as I love everyone, I can sense a vibe that they wonder why I am there. They look like they would rather not see me. I never see a black person at the earlier services. That is the feeling that I got when I started going here. I feel like with the earlier services, they need to knock down the racial tension wall. I do feel it sometimes. You can feel that they don't want you there. I don't feel hatred, but I don't know another word for it.

Some of the people we interviewed stated that some people in the earlier services speak negatively about the 11 o'clock service. Some of the people in the other services don't consider the noon service a real service.

Interviewer: How do you know that people think that?
White member: I have heard them say it.
Interviewer: Why do you think that people think that?
White member: It's because we are different. It's full of different music, we sing different songs and have different sermons.

Interestingly, two of the white people we interviewed stated that they felt the 11 o'clock service was less accepting of whites. One of these respondents no longer attends the church because of this feeling.

In the secular world is not OK to be white, especially because of the emphasis on diversity. The church took that same attitude. If I didn't praise the same way the black people did. . . . I am not loud and demonstrative. Black people are out voicing everything. They would say African Americans really know how to praise God. It's not a white way; it's just my way. They didn't praise the differences; they just put us down because we weren't like them. I would still be there, but it is more the attitude of the administration. In order to be politically correct, they told white people they weren't doing things right. They went out of their way to over-accommodate people who were black and Hispanic. It's a multicultural church. They needed to show up and present the Word of God and give people the translation. They didn't need to focus on our color. It was a very big focus for them.

This seems to be a minority view among the white people at the 11 o'-clock service. Most were very positive about the emphasis on diversity.

It is interesting that a significant number of black and Hispanic members felt rejected and looked down upon by white members who attend the other services, but they did not appear to feel the same rejection by the white members of the 11 o'clock service. These white members at the 11 o'clock service were drawn from the earlier services and come from the same class backgrounds, yet not one black or Hispanic respondent reported a negative "vibe" or attitude from the white members of the integrated service.

One explanation for this could be that white members who committed to the 11 o'clock service are much more open to embracing people of different ethnicities than the people from the earlier services. Another explanation, however, could be that the difference is not with the individual white members at the different services, but rather that the social environments of the two services are different. Black and Hispanic respondents describe the environment of earlier services as "stiff," "reserved," and "stuck-up." They describe the 11 o'clock service as being "warm," "informal," and "comfortable." The visible class differences between the earlier services and the 11 o'clock service, combined with the more reserved ways of interacting among white people, probably contribute to an impression that the earlier services are cold, rejecting, and aloof. The presence of black and Hispanic members in large numbers, and the intentional efforts of whites to be welcoming, at the 11 o'clock service seems to produce a very different social environment.

Another source of tension between the services is the impression among some 11 o'clock attenders that their service is a "second-class citizen" that gets less attention and resources from the staff. Particularly discouraging for some is that the 11 o'clock service does not have Sunday school classes for children. Families are encouraged to take their children to Sunday school at the earlier services and bring them to the 11 o'clock church service. Child care for small children is provided at the 11 o'clock service, but all of the children are put into one room. Most of the volunteers for child care come from the earlier services. A number of respondents complained about this.

> Interviewer: Do you have any frustrations about church?
> Hispanic member: Actually, the only part that I wish they had was Sunday school for the kids. They only have one and the earlier services have Sunday school classes for all the little kids. But we have only one. I would like my daughter to be in a Sunday school class . . . it's either day care or worship.

Some also mentioned that the child care volunteers from the other services seemed less enthusiastic about serving the 11 o'clock children.

> I felt like the eleven service wasn't valued as much. People wanted to see it go because it was so much more work. Then, I saw how hard they worked on the other services too. By the time the eleven service comes around, the child care people are really frustrated and tired. I first felt that eleven service people were unwelcome. People now know that we are not going away and we get extra help. (Filipina)

This highlights an interesting dynamic at Brookside. The white middle-class members provide most of the financial resources and volunteer assistance to allow the 11 o'clock service to operate. The salaries of the 11 o'clock pastors and worship leaders are drawn from the overall church budget, which relies heavily on contributions from the large numbers of white middle-class members in the earlier services. In addition, the leaders of many of the community outreach activities and the volunteers for child care come from the earlier services. Yet it appears to many who attend the 11 o'clock service that theirs is getting shortchanged because they have less resources for child care and Sunday school than the other services. This leads to the impression that the 11 o'clock service isn't as highly valued by the church.

This dynamic prompted one white 11 o'clock attender to suggest that they draw more from their own resources.

I think that we are the last service of the day, so the people helping out get tired. The eleven service stands out differently. I think we ought to take care of our own needs once we have been established longer. We need to start pulling from our own resources. (White)

The way the preaching rotation is handled also contributes to the impression among some that the 11 o'clock service is less valued. Mike and the other white pastors alternate the preaching in the 11 o'clock service with Rod and Luis. However, Rod and Luis rarely preach or lead prayers in the earlier services. A number of respondents felt that it should be a two-way street—the earlier services should be exposed to different types of preaching just as the integrated service is.

In addition, a number of our respondents shared their perception that the white pastors "water down" their sermons in the 11 o'clock service, making them less challenging spiritually and intellectually than the sermons in the earlier services.

I enjoy the teaching, but sometimes I really think they hold back at 11. Maybe they are afraid that people won't understand. It's strange because once in a while you get a service on Sunday where it's deep and where we can grow. But, then we go all light and topical. It's really frustrating. I don't know if it's for the new people they are trying to bring up slowly or what. (Hispanic)

In Sunday school people will comment about what the pastor said and I didn't get that at the 11 o'clock service. I miss out on what the 9:30 people are hearing. It's like they change the sermon for the eleven service. (Hispanic)

Interviewer: What do you enjoy about being at the 11 o'clock service at Brookside?

Hispanic member: The worship is good. The teaching I don't really like.

Interviewer: What about it don't you like?

Hispanic member: It's the downfall of the eleven service. It seems like the teaching is quite shallow if you are an older Christian. Sometimes I feel like I am starving. I bring my friends here and we don't get fed.

Since the pastors preaching at the 11 o'clock service often do try to make their sermons more palatable to people who have little experience with church, people who desire more challenging sermons are left feeling unsatisfied. Some see this as further evidence that the people at the 11 o'clock service aren't as valued as the others.

Many at the 11 o'clock service would like to see a reciprocal relationship between the services, where the predominantly white services could benefit and be challenged by the different perspectives and different worship styles of the 11 o'clock service. They feel that this would also lead to less tension and more understanding between the services.

> My frustration is that the whole church doesn't mirror the eleven service. That's what the community is . . . just like the eleven service. There are long traditions of values and histories of being only one way. It takes time to break barriers of tradition. (African American)

Mike Van Egan shares this sentiment and hopes that all three services will eventually look like the 11 o'clock service. But he stresses that it is a slow transformation that will take years, maybe decades. Rod and Luis attend the other services as well and sometimes lead prayer and occasionally preach. Occasionally the African American worship leader will lead a song or two in a more upbeat style. But Mike wants to be careful not to alienate longtime members and wants to make sure they don't feel like they are "losing their church." Mike gives the analogy of turning an airplane around in mid-flight: "if you turn it around by doing a 180-degree turn everyone is going to be jolted out of their seats. But if you turn it around slowly without any sudden turns it will happen more smoothly." Mike states that when the 11 o'clock service began in 1997 the other services were 95 percent white. Now they are 88 percent white. He hopes that in another ten years they will be 78 percent white. Thus, his vision is one of a slow transformation to a completely interracial congregation, with the 11 o'clock service playing the leading role in that transformation.

Learning from This Case

The case of Brookside Community Church illustrates the difficulty of racially integrating a predominantly white church, even when the surrounding community is mostly non-white, and even when the pastors have well-thought-out strategies to integrate the services. This church has chosen to use one of its three services as a model toward which the other services will eventually move over a long period of time. This "turning the plane around slowly" strategy is designed to transform the church into a more racially and ethnically inclusive organization without alienating its predominantly white middle-class constituency.

This church is similar to both Wilcrest and Crosstown in that the motivation for becoming racially diverse was the changing demographics of the neighborhood in which it resides. In all three cases, keeping the white constituency committed to the church has been a key obstacle to maintaining diversity. Brookside's approach to this dilemma differs from that of the other two; Brookside has chosen to keep two of three services culturally white and to ask a group of whites to intentionally commit to the multi-ethnic service for a set length of time. The need to continually replenish the numbers of white members committing to the 11 o'clock service highlights the difficulty of preventing "white flight" once the church becomes diverse.

Brookside is also similar to Wilcrest in that existing non-white members played a key role in the transition process. At Wilcrest, some of the few pre-transition non-Anglo members were outgoing people who made sure that new non-white visitors felt welcome. Others took it upon themselves to start ministries and programs to welcome non-white members. At Brookside, Mike Van Egan specifically asked all of the existing non-white members to commit to leadership positions in the new multi-ethnic service. It appears that, at least in the context of a transition from a predominantly white organization to an integrated organization, key minority group members can have a large impact on the success of the transition process.

The strategies used in the 11 o'clock service that were designed to make it more attractive to members of the surrounding community seem to be working. Attendance at the service continues to grow, and almost all of this growth has come from the surrounding community. The service is led by a diverse leadership team, which includes the three dominant groups (white, black, Hispanic) the service seeks to combine. The musical styles used in worship are diverse, combining gospel, contemporary Christian, and Latin rhythms, sung in English and in Spanish. Sermons are preached by a diverse pastoral team and are delivered in very different cultural styles. The leadership intentionally puts a diverse group of people up front to perform the tasks of the service. These intentional strategies have made the church feel like "home" to its black and Latino members as well as to non-white visitors.

Given the experience of Crosstown, the question remains whether the white presence at the 11 o'clock service will dwindle, or whether the staff will be able to secure enough commitments from white members to keep white numbers stable. As we have seen in the other cases, white people seem to have a greater tendency to expect things to reflect their interests and desires within a religious organization than do other ethnic groups. This is probably a result of their predominance in the larger society, where things are typically done according to white norms and standards. This makes it difficult to integrate a religious organization without losing the white members of the congregation.

The leadership of Brookside is keenly aware of this challenge and has therefore adopted a strategy of "turning the plane around slowly" rather than a rapid transformation in the way things are done. This tactic has been successful in retaining the white constituency, but it also seems to be causing tensions among the various services. Those attending the 11 o'-clock service, particularly blacks and Hispanics, wonder why the rest of the church is not being challenged and blessed by the diversity of styles in their service. They also wonder why their service seems to get fewer resources in terms of volunteers and programs for kids.

The strategy of leadership asking some white members to make a three-year commitment to the 11 o'clock service is interesting. It suggests that not enough white people in the congregation are naturally drawn to the 11 o'clock service to retain a significant white presence there, and that they need to be prodded to make a commitment. After their three-year commitment, many return to the earlier services. Some, however, stay and seem to be transformed by the experience. A significant number of white members said that they would not want to return to an all-white service. This group of whites suggest that there is hope for a full integration of the entire church body into a multi-ethnic church without completely eliminating white people from the ranks.

Perhaps the most striking finding in this case is the importance of creating a warm, embracing environment in the congregation. The pastors of this service all seem to have a gift for embracing people and making them feel welcome. They have also made a strong effort to connect with people and to physically reach out to them during the services. The diversity of the people in the pews also seems to generate an atmosphere of warmth and acceptance. A number of people, particularly the Hispanic members we interviewed, stated that just seeing the different faces of the diverse congregation made them feel accepted and made the church feel like "home." This is an interesting statement—one would think that seeing only members of one's own ethnicity would make people feel more at home than would a diverse environment. But many of these people have grown up in diverse neighborhoods, have attended diverse schools, and work in diverse settings. Many of them are also involved in racially mixed families. For them, "home" is a very diverse place.

This dynamic is very similar to what we have seen in each of the previous cases. In all of the congregations we have examined so far, the diversity of the church made non-whites feel welcome. Those in interracial marriages also reported a feeling of "home" where they and their children could fit in. Brookside is also similar to Wilcrest and Crosstown in that they all seem to have prioritized creating a warm and welcoming environment, which has succeeded in drawing a diverse crowd. Working to create this warm and loving environment seems to be key to the functioning of integrated religious organizations. A central obstacle at Messiah was a lack of a feeling of embrace by numerical minorities.

The feeling of home experienced by members of Brookside's 11 o'clock service contrasts sharply with the feeling many black and Hispanic members get when they enter the church's predominantly white services and activities. Many report that they felt rejected, judged, and unwelcome in these places. Conversely, they do not seem to feel this way when they come into contact with the white people in the 11 o'clock service, which is still more than a third white—even though the white people who attend the 11 o'clock service are drawn primarily from the other (predominantly white) services.

We think the best explanation for this apparent anomaly is that the dynamics of social interaction in a large group of white people are quite different from those dynamics in a mixed group of whites, blacks, and Hispanics. In other words, the rejection that black and Hispanic members experience when they enter the all-white services may be due to the group dynamics of the social environment itself, not to rejecting or prejudiced white individuals.

The differences in social environment between the 11 o'clock service and the earlier services are immediately noticeable upon entering into the sanctuary. In the all-white services, people are less likely to make eye contact, greet, or hug you as you enter. The social norms of interaction among white people, particularly upper-middle-class white people, seem to be characterized by more reserve, more formality, and less expression of affection compared to black and Hispanic communities. If true, this would explain, at least partially, the fact that black and Hispanic members of the 11 o'clock service do not feel rejected and ignored by the white people at the 11 o'clock service—the norms of social interaction in the 11 o'clock service are simply different. Smiles, eye contact, and physical touching are more the norm there, and the white people in the service may have adjusted to this norm. Even if the white people have not adjusted, the dominant numbers of Hispanics make their ways of interaction more the norm of the group. In contrast, the rules of engagement in the other services are dominated by white norms—lack of eye contact, reserve, formality, and less physical touching in the form of hugs and handshakes.

If all of this is true, it suggests that the simple raw numbers of people from various ethnic groups can powerfully affect the social environment of a group, which in turn powerfully affects the experiences of those entering that group. This also suggests that in predominantly white environments, blacks and Hispanics will tend to feel rejected independent of the intentions of the white people in that group, making it difficult to integrate all-white religious organizations.

It is also probable that some middle-class white members of the other services really do feel superior to the black and Hispanic members of the 11 o'clock service and would rather not see them around their church. This sense of superiority might have as much to do with class as with race. Even if only a relatively small percentage of white people felt this way, the large numbers of white people at this church would ensure that the black and Hispanic members would come into contact with them eventually. And a few bad experiences of rejection can often negate a large number of positive interactions.

Overall, the findings in this case are consistent with a number of findings from the others we have considered. The spiritual benefits of worshiping in a diverse environment, the importance of creating a warm and friendly environment, and the potential threat of "white flight" were all present here. This case is unique, however, in the way the church approached these issues structurally. The "church within a church" format seems to ameliorate relational isolation among numerical minorities and to keep "white flight" at bay. What will happen as the plane continues to turn and the diversity of the church begins to affect the other services remains an open question.

6

Together and Separate

Thus far we have focused on churches. However, in this chapter we examine the barriers to racial integration within a university student religious organization, Christ in Action. This case expands our understanding of the dynamics of interracial religious organizations in three key ways. Unlike churches, student religious organizations have, by definition, temporary memberships. Moreover, members of these religious organizations typically also are members of churches; the student religious organizations serve as spiritual and social supplements to their church. Furthermore, college is a time and place where people are open to exploring different identities and experimenting with new situations. Given these conditions, we might expect members' investments in or commitments to these kinds of religious organizations to be weaker than that of church members, and the organizations may not be central to members' sense of belonging. Further, members may be more tolerant of conflict or unmet preferences.

The Christ in Action group we studied is on the campus of South Urban University. South Urban University is an elite private university located in the sprawling city of Houston. Drawing upon its diverse location and its highly selective admissions process, South Urban's undergraduate student body is 34 percent non-white. A primary focus of South Urban is providing an excellent undergraduate education; the university ranks among the top schools in the country. In accordance with its concentration on academics, South Urban University has no social fraternities. However, there are approximately 230 student organizations on campus with an eclectic variety of interests and purposes. These include drama, academics, sports, juggling, social activism, and religion, among many others. One of these organizations is Christ in Action.

Christ in Action is an international Christian student organization based in the United States. Founded in the 1950s, it has since expanded to nearly 1,110 college campuses in the United States and worldwide. The organization is also interdenominational. However, based upon its own statement of faith and mission, the organization is clearly located within the evangelical Christian tradition. The original intent of the founders was to "win the campus today and change the world tomorrow." Today, this primarily includes "[turning] lost [college] students into Christ-centered laborers," "lost" students being those who do not have a "relationship with God through Jesus Christ." Christ in Action purposes "to see students embrace the purpose, love and forgiveness that God offers them in a relationship with Jesus Christ." The group bases its mission on the Bible, which it believes is the inerrant, "infallible Written Word" of God that is "uniquely . . . inspired by the Holy Spirit."

Most local Christ in Action chapters are directed by college-educated paid staff members. Staff is responsible for coordinating and leading weekly Bible studies as well as other events, such as evangelism and social activities. They also train student members of the organization in evangelical Christian theology, practice, evangelism, and leadership using a standard training program developed by the organization. Students are gradually promoted to leadership within their local organizations as they move through the training program. By their junior and senior years students are given leadership responsibilities, which include leading small Bible study groups of freshmen and sophomores. Students also participate in the coordination of the organization. In addition to leading the weekly Bible studies, they help plan and organize weekly Bible studies and social and evangelistic events, and they participate in the training of fellow students in Christian theology and practice.

This traditional structure has attracted primarily white students. In response to the increasing ethnic and racial diversity of college campuses over the past fifteen years, Christ in Action has developed three ethnicity-specific campus organizations. The intent of these organizations is to reach ethnic and racial minorities with the "gospel." However, although the statements of faith and mission of these groups are the same as that of Christ in Action, their structure and organization are developed to accommodate the cultural preferences and needs of ethnic and racial minorities.

In this chapter, we examine the role of both interracial and race-specific groups within the Christ in Action organization on South Urban University's campus. We talked with thirty undergraduate students of various races and ethnicities who are members of these groups. This study demonstrates the importance and effectiveness of racially homogeneous groups within racially diverse religious organizations. Moreover, it provides a unique perspective on racial diversity within religious organizations, particularly because these respondents are young, highly religious students on a secular university campus. As such, we would expect them to be more progressive on issues of race as compared with others within evangelical Christianity.

Christ in Action at South Urban University

South Urban University has both an interracial Christ in Action group and one race-specific group, Reach, on campus. About fifty undergraduate students participate in the interracial Christ in Action weekly activities. In terms of race, 45 percent of the students are Asian (this includes Indians), 45 percent are white, and the few remaining students are Latino or African American. A large group Bible study and small group Bible studies are the organizations' core activities. Both the large group Bible study and the small group Bible studies meet weekly. The weekly large group Bible study is open to all regular attenders and newcomers. One of the respondents describes it as "church with a bunch of young people." There is a time for singing, teaching, and games during each meeting. One of the three Christ in Action staff members for South Urban University does the teaching and students lead the singing and games. The small group Bible studies are organized by gender, class level (i.e., freshman, sophomore, etc.) and dormitory. For example, two small group Bible studies may be held in one of the dormitories, one for freshman men specifically and the other for freshman women. There are usually six or seven people in each small group. Other regularly scheduled activities include leadership meetings, socials, and evangelistic events.

Reach is the race-specific Christ in Action organization for African Americans. On South Urban's campus, Reach has about fifteen students. Reach is led primarily by student leaders. They organize activities, facilitate Bible studies, and spiritually mentor other students in the group. Unlike the traditional Christ in Action, Reach has no weekly large group meeting of its own. The core Reach activities are small group Bible studies. There are two groups, one for women and one for men. Periodically, the two small group Bible studies meet together. Students also get together for prayer meetings and evangelistic activities, such as "witnessing" (i.e., sharing the Christian message with non-Christians), feeding the homeless, and working with inner-city youth.

Although Reach is formally a part of Christ in Action, practically speaking it functions separately on campus—so much so that some of the students we interviewed were unsure whether Reach was a part of Christ in Action. Christ in Action staff have little involvement in the organization and direction of Reach. Christ in Action's main role is providing Reach with supplies and other resources.

Student Life in Christ in Action

We conducted thirty interviews with both Christ in Action and Reach members (8 white, 6 African American, 12 Asian, 2 Hispanic, and 2 mixed race). Twenty-six of the students we spoke with participate in Christ in Action and six participate in Reach (two African American students participate in both groups).

Ten of the respondents in Christ in Action attend the weekly large group Bible study and nineteen students are involved in a small group Bible study. One third of the students participate in other leadership meetings and more than half attend the social events. However, the involvement of the students appears to be polarized. Half of the students who participate in Christ in Action activities are moderately involved, by which we mean that they attend the large group Bible study or a small group Bible study once a week. The other half are very involved attending some kind of Christ in Action activity at least four times a week. To demonstrate the level of involvement of these students, here is what a few of the interviewees told us about their weekly Christ in Action participation.

> So, right now, I lead the Praise Team. So, because of that, I'm on the leadership team. Our leadership team meets once a week on Sunday nights for about an hour. Then we have a weekly men's leaders Bible study, and that's on Tuesday morning from about 7:30 to about 8:30 or so. We have leaders' meeting every other Thursday, just for all leaders, male and female, and that's over Thursday dinner. And I lead a Bible study, so we meet on Fridays from about 5:00 to 6:30. And then we have our large group meeting which is from 9 to 10 on Thursday evening. (Asian)

I go to a girls' [small group] Bible study. I lead a freshmen [small group] Bible study. I go to the Christ in Action weekly [large group] Bible studies. And then [I] go to a Christ in Action leadership team meeting. And sometimes, every other week, we have another leaders' meeting. (White)

Basically there's a leadership team meeting, [usually on] Sunday nights. . . . We talk . . . about what we want to do during Christ in Action large group Bible study. And I'm basically in charge of socials, and so I try to come up with . . . ideas that Christ in Action [members] can do together. And then there's a meeting on Thursdays, the large group Bible study and we have socials on Friday nights where we go out to dinner and perhaps something else. (Latino)

As we can see, these students are committed to Christ in Action. They give several hours per week to Christ in Action activities. In addition to attending both the large group Bible study and a small group Bible study, they lead other small group Bible studies and attend leadership and planning meetings. Furthermore, there are students from every racial group (except African American) who are very involved participants in Christ in Action activities. The level of students' participation is likely a reflection of the Christ in Action training program as most of the very involved students are upperclassmen. Nonetheless, group activities consume a large part of their life

However, despite high levels of commitment among these Christ in Action members, five of the twelve very involved students have considered leaving the organization. Three of these five students are white. When asked if she ever considering leaving Christ in Action, one of the white students replied:

Oh, definitely. Yeah, I would say at some of the low points, maybe. I can't remember the particular time off the top of my head, but there've just been times, especially with evangelistic techniques . . . where I was just really fed up and I didn't feel like this was me or what the Lord was calling me to do. And I wondered why am I even in this and I thought about switching over to Christian Connection, but I have an overwhelming sense every time that God has put me in Christ in Action for a reason and even if I didn't particularly agree I needed to be there and deal with the fact that I didn't agree rather than like run away. (White)

Evangelism is central to the mission of Christ in Action and students are strongly encouraged to share the Christian message with non-Christian students. Although this student is not opposed to evangelism, she does not agree with *how* Christ in Action expects students to evangelize other students. Moreover, she does not feel "called" to participate in these evangelism activities. As a result, she considered leaving the organization to begin attending another Christian campus organization, Christian Connection. Christian Connection is a predominantly white Christian organization on South Urban's campus. Similar to Christ in Action, Christian Connection has weekly large group and small group Bible studies. However, it has a less assertive evangelism agenda than Christ in Action. Nonetheless, she has remained in Christ in Action because she believes God has a purpose for her in Christ in Action.

Another white student also considered leaving Christ in Action to become involved in Christian Connection. He felt he might have a better chance of leading worship during the large group Bible study in Christian Connection and might develop closer friendships.

> Yeah, I've thought about [leaving]. A lot of times it's for selfish reasons. "Oh wow, I could do worship at Christian Connection and make good friends" or something like that. I wouldn't wanna do that. I wouldn't wanna sacrifice something that I've worked so hard on just because of something like that. I feel like, it serves my needs, but if I stick with it I'm better off that way and in that direction. Also as I grow into leadership, I can help with that and work on some areas that are changing. (White)

Although he does not say it, this student's feelings about his chances to lead worship in Christ in Action could, in part, be because the worship leader for the Christ in Action large group Bible studies has for the last four years been an Asian student. However, the current worship leader is a senior. His decision to stay in Christ in Action may be motivated by a perceived opportunity to move into leadership and become the next praise leader.

Time is also a factor in students' decisions to leave or remain in Christ in Action. One of the very active Asian students tells us that the activities are very time-consuming. However, she has decided to remain in the group because the friendship and spiritual growth she gains outweigh the time she has had to sacrifice.

Yeah, when it became really time-consuming. And with any organization . . . I think you have problems. So sometimes yeah, I had to think
about it. But I didn't want to miss the challenge and the fellowship I
guess and the way I grow and the way it stimulates me, so it was worth
staying. (Southeast Asian)

Overall, a slight majority of the students who participate in Christ
in Action (fifteen of the twenty-six) have at one time or another considered leaving. Moderately active students similarly offered that they
were uncomfortable with the evangelism strategy of Christ in Action
and that time constraints were an issue. Other reasons they cited were
disagreements with Christ in Action's theology and its organizational
structure.

Given the level of commitment among students in the traditional
Christ in Action group, we might expect the group members to have close
relationships within the group. Many students reported that their friends
in Christ in Action were "definitely" their closest. However, as alluded to
by one interviewee above, Christ in Action is not the primary resource for
friendship for a number of students in the traditional group. Among the
twenty-four students we interviewed in the interracial Christ in Action
group, just over half reported that their closest friends are in Christ in Action.

For students who reported that their closest friends were outside of
Christ in Action, living arrangement seems to influence who their closest
friends are. Here is what some of them shared:

I think that I have a group of friends, I wouldn't call them close friends
because I don't really do anything with them outside of the Bible study
itself. . . . My roommate, though, is one of my closer friends, I mean he
goes to the Bible study, but I think it's more because he's my roommate
as opposed to being from Christ in Action. (Asian)

My closest group of friends would be the people I live with, none of
whom are involved with Christ in Action. (Latina)

Consistent with what respondents told us about their personal social ties
to Christ in Action, just under two-thirds report that relationships, overall, are not particularly close.

It's a pretty inviting environment. . . . It's a little bit better than just acquaintances, but it's certainly not close friends. I mean, it's a gathering of people with similar beliefs, so there's a degree of camaraderie. (Latina)

They're pretty close, on a religious level. And on a social level, it depends. Some of them, some are people that live together, so that helps their relationship. . . . On a social level, outside of small group, sometimes we talk, but not too much I guess. (White)

Another student who is very involved in the group and considers her Christ in Action friends to be her closest friends similarly describes the overall closeness of people within the group as not particularly close.

I think they're really good for as close as you can be in such a large group. I know that people are closer within their classes and within their colleges, but I think that's normal. But for the most part it's very friendly, people talk to everyone. That's good. (Asian)

Moreover, in cases where relationships are described as strong or close, the closeness has not come easily. A white woman in her senior year explained that during "senior year we tried really hard to create a strong sense of community with our study and just prayed about it a lot and I think to a great extent I saw it come about more than I have in other years."

Although a few students told us that the overall relationships are very close or very good in Christ in Action, most support the descriptions given above. The relationships are merely "pretty good" or good enough. People are close religiously, but not socially. Other social ties seem to be more important for students than social ties within the group. Closer friendships tend to be organized around similar residence or college major more than around participation in Christ in Action. Moreover, the closeness that does exist within the group has admittedly taken some work.

Among the Asian students who reported that their closest friends were in Christ in Action, four explained that other Asian students in Christ in Action attend their church, Greater Metro Asian Church (GMAC), a predominantly Asian congregation, and that they are all actively involved in the college group at church. Their closest friendship ties are with other students who attend their church college group and who also attend Christ in Action.

> Yeah, actually a good group of my friends from Christ in Action also overlap with my church. My church fellowship has about thirty South Urban people in it. . . . And I'd say about fifteen to twenty of those people come to Christ in Action. They are definitely my very close friends. (Asian)

Another Asian student who also attends this church put it this way:

> My closest friends are in Christ in Action but . . . I'd rather say my closest friends are in my church, but they also happen to be in Christ in Action. (Asian)

GMAC is a vital resource for developing close relationships among the Asian students. At least for one student, GMAC is a more important source for friendship ties than Christ in Action. The bonds created within this environment have carried over into Christ in Action. Furthermore, three of the four students are leaders in Christ in Action as well. However, much as we saw at Messiah, the closeness among the Asian students does not go unnoticed by other members of Christ in Action. Half of the white students we spoke with expressed some concerns about the close relationships among the Asian Christ in Action members. The Asian students appear to be "cliquish" and separate from the rest of the group. Although these students are not in favor of "cliques" within the group generally, the Asian "clique" is of particular concern to them.

> I was overwhelmed with the amount of Asian people. I have never seen that many Asian people in my life. . . . There's definitely an Asian sphere and a non-Asian sphere of people, which is disconcerting to me. There are a lot of them that all go to the same church and there's almost this, I don't know. They're just naturally good friends with each other. . . . Their friendship groups are seemingly becoming almost exclusively Asian. (White)

> I guess that was probably one of the initial things I noticed about Christ in Action was how many Asians there are. . . . They are tending to stay in their own ethnic groups. I know that that's kind of been a hindrance

to some people. . . . I've talked to people who view Christ in Action as like an organization for Christian Asians, not just Christians in general or whatever. (White)

Both of these students appear to have had little previous exposure to Asians, at least in large numbers. One even admits to having been "overwhelmed" by them. Furthermore, the proportion of Asians in the group and the close friendship bonds among some of them seems exclusive to these non-Asian members. Not only do people within the group feel excluded; the Asians' presence has also come to be seen by some as a "hindrance" to newcomers because the group has a reputation of being "an organization for Christian Asians." This despite the significantly higher likelihood among white students to have their closest friends in the group (see table 6.1). Furthermore, a racial dichotomy of Asians and non-Asians has formed, which is "disconcerting" to many whites. Although there is an equal proportion of white students in the group, it appears that this is still not sufficient for them to feel they have ownership of the group. As Tatum (1997) notes, white people, as the dominant group, take their own homogeneous grouping as the unexamined norm but are threatened by the homogeneous groupings of minorities in interracial settings. This dynamic seems to be playing itself out here.

However, whites are not the only people who notice the closeness among certain Asian students. Other Asians, who do not attend the Asian church, describe their friendship group as "cliquish." For these Asian students, the "Asian clique" is something that should be avoided. One Asian student told us that she believes "cliques" are a hindrance to spreading the Christian message, regardless of their basis. Evangelism should take priority over friendship group preferences:

Yeah, I feel like it shouldn't be that way because if you just remain within your comfort zone, whether it's your Christian community or your Asian Christian community, the Gospel is not going to get out of that community, and how are you supposed to shine for God or be a good example for Him if you don't enter other groups in the real world, a world that is made of Christians and non-Christians? (Asian)

Another Asian student, who is originally from Malaysia, also believes people should transcend their comfort zones. However, she offers a more personal explanation for this belief:

TABLE 6.1

Analysis of Location of Closest Friends for Christ in Action Interracial Group Members (n = 24)—Inside the Group or Outside the Group?

	Non-White Members	White Members
#1 closest friend is inside group	53	67
#2 closest friend is inside group	53	89+
#3 closest friend is inside group	47	89+
Mean # of 3 closest friends who are inside group	1.67	2.44+

NOTES: Pearson's Chi-Square test (+ p < .1, * p < .05, ** p < .01). Does not include members of Reach.

TABLE 6.2

Percentage of Closest Friends within the Christ in Action Interracial Group Who Are the Same Race as the Respondent (n = 24)

	Non-White Members	White Members
#1 within-group friend same race	47	33
#2 within-group friend same race	60	56
#3 within-group friend same race	40	67
Mean # of 3 closest friends within the group who are the same race	1.86	1.56

NOTES: Pearson's Chi-Square test (+ p < .1, * p < .05, ** p < .01) Does not include members of Reach.

The only reason why I didn't join Christ in Action initially was because the whole Asian clique was there. And, I didn't want to be part of the Asian clique [laughs] because I wanted to hang around more with other people. I'm not saying that I won't have Asian friends, but I just don't want to be . . . they keep to themselves. . . . It doesn't make sense for me, because I came all the way here [from Malaysia], and I should try to get to know more people here instead of just do what I'm more comfortable with. Now I actually feel pretty comfortable with Caucasians . . . I mean, I have Asian friends. I don't know where this is leading me to [laughter], but basically yeah I just didn't want to be exclusive in that manner, if you know what I'm saying. (Asian)

This student believes that she should make friends with other people since she is not from this country. She does not mean by this that she should make friends with people from any racial or ethnic background different from her own—she is speaking about whites specifically. Furthermore, it is such a priority for her to integrate with whites that she is willing to endure the discomfort she experiences among white students (*"now*, I actually feel pretty comfortable with [whites]") and to sacrifice an opportunity to develop friendships with other Asian students.

Many of the students in Christ in Action are very involved in the organization, in some cases committing more than ten hours a week to its activities. They regularly interact with one another and, as a result, develop close relationships with others in the group. However, for non-whites, high commitment and involvement in the group have not necessarily translated to students having their closest friendships within the group. Although most non-white students report having close friends in Christ in Action, less than half say these are their closest friends. Furthermore, ties to a church congregation are important for a sense of belonging, particularly among some of the Asian students. These respondents have friends in Christ in Action who also attend the same predominantly Asian church, an overlap that leads to dense friendships networks. Among students who are not apart of this friendship group, the tight relationship bonds among Asian students are perceived as cliquish and exclusionary.

Student Life in Reach

We interviewed six Reach students in Christ in Action. All six students are actively involved in Reach. Each attends a Reach small group Bible study weekly and participates in other Reach activities such as prayer, social gatherings, and evangelism events. And unlike Christ in Action, the regular interaction these students experience in Reach promotes very close relationships among them and other Reach members.

> We're like just brothers in Christ . . . we talk about life, we talk about ambitions, post-grad, you know, whatever. (African-American)

> [The Reach Bible study] is the thing that most of us look forward to during the week. It's like a study break. It's a release. During the week it's hard to go to church so women's Bible study is a good time to meet and get encouragement [and] encourage others. (African-American)

> They take the place of my family. I was a homebody when I was in high school. I never really left home. . . . I just loved my family. . . . Coming to South Urban and not having that and also not having my church

family from Dallas, as well. . . . So Reach took over all of that. (African-American)

Only one student told us that his closest friends are not in Reach. His closest friends are actually in Christian Connection, another campus group similar in purpose to Christ in Action. However, his Reach relationships are still very important.

> Most of the people that I'm around in my college are in Christian Connection. So I'm around them a little bit more than my friends from Reach. . . . But the leader of Reach last semester, he graduated. . . . He's kind of like a mentor, that's a little bit different than just a friend. He's like a mentor. I really look up to him. . . . And then the leader [of Reach] this semester, I really look up to him. It's almost like, not just a friendship, but I kinda look up to them. I wanna grow like them. (African American)

This student still values his relationships in Reach, particularly with older male members. He describes their relationships as "not just [friendships]." They are his mentors. He admires them and desires to emulate them. Hence, although Reach is not an important resource for peer relationships for this respondent, it is still an important resource for very close friendships.

Reach students also regularly get together outside of formal activities like Bible study and prayer. They go out to eat, gather for parties, and buy each other gifts.

> We're like really good friends with pretty much all the guys in men's Reach. A lot of times they'll surprise us with different things. Like, they'll randomly bring flowers to us. Valentine's Day they always give us something. . . . Or we'll like bake cookies or something for them. (African American)

> I would have to say the thing I enjoy the most is being around these people, because I don't think there's any substitute for that. The people are so warm and caring though, and a lot of times we'll actually go and spend time together outside of Bible studies or outside of meetings or whatever . . . we'll all go out and go get some hot wings or . . . we had like a little party at [one of the leader's] house,

you know, and it's just fellowship with other believers. (African American)

Compared to Christ in Action, Reach is more fundamental to the quality of its members' social and religious lives on South Urban's campus. All but one of them reported that their closest friendships are with other people in Reach. The student who said his closest peer friendships were not in Reach still had very close relationships with other people in Reach. Members draw upon one another for support and share their life goals and dreams with one another. The group serves as a surrogate family for some; for others it is a social space where they can bond with other African American Christians. For black men, the experience of having close relationships with other African American Christian men is particularly important. Members also regularly socialize outside of the Bible studies and participate in other school activities together, such as the Give God the Praise gospel choir and the Black Student Organization.

Is Reach a Good Thing?

According to nearly all of the students we interviewed, racial diversity is beneficial for Christians. Students believe this across racial groups. Reasons given for their beliefs are both religious and personal. Christians are supposed to be "united" across race. Racial diversity increases the opportunity of religious organizations to spread the Christian message to more people. It is a "witness" to non-Christians. In other words, racial diversity demonstrates that, through Christianity, social barriers can be overcome. Additionally, respondents reported that they believe racial diversity improves their understanding of others and others' cultures, and that racial diversity provides them with the opportunity to see how other Christians express their faith.

Interviewer: What benefits do you see from having the diversity . . . in Christ in Action?

Asian student: I think the experiences and viewpoints that people have to contribute. Just being able to understand what other cultures are like and see how people of other cultures will view religion, and how they can contribute to that movement just to "Go therefore and make disciples of the nations." . . . Being able to see people of various colors intermingling and worshiping together just as one body, I hope that's an example to non-believers also, to see people coming together because of a common love that exists.

One of the things . . . that I learned [is] people are still people. On the surface he seems different but he's still a human just like I am, you know? The cliché if you prick them they'll bleed kinda thing. It's comforting I think to realize that as different as this person may seem from you, he's still just like you. And I think also, because [there is] . . . prejudice all over the world, when non-Christians see that you're crossing over these barriers that usually divide people they're gonna . . . want to know how come that black person can hang out with an Asian person. You know? I think it can be used as subtle witnessing. (African American)

I feel like we have a lot to teach each other and I feel like seeing all the different ways that people experience God and experience their faith really opens our eyes to what a global God we serve, and just how far-reaching he is and just how many ways there are to adequately glorify God. It doesn't have to be this one-way thing that all these churches do. You know? There's tons of ways to worship God, I think. (White)

If the body of God is not united, then nothing else will be. . . . The body of God is supposed to be one and it's not. If there was one organization that was united even though it's diverse it should be a Christian organization. So I think that it's a good witness to a lot of other people outside too. (Asian)

However, if racial diversity is beneficial for Christians and Christian organizations, is there a place for race- or ethnicity-specific groups among Christians? We asked our interviewees to share their thoughts on whether groups such as Reach can be beneficial. The modal response students give to this question begins something like this: "I support groups like Reach, but. . . ." Some of these students recognize that Reach is beneficial for those who are in the group, but at the same time they would like to see African American students integrate with the larger Christ in Action group. Many individuals explain that having more African Americans in the group would personally improve their own experience in Christ in Action. One of the Asian students commented:

I think [Reach] has been really good. I wish I could have seen much more of [the people in Reach] and have been more involved in their lives and everything. But, just looking at their ministry and just seeing how strong they are and that they're going through the same experience. . . . [But], I think it's better for us to be involved as a group, just for more unification. I mean there are just so many cool people out there that I wanna get to know and when we're in separate places and we're so involved in our own little group, it's hard to like really get to know people on more of a deeper level and have this kind of friendships. And so I wish sometimes that it was like we were more involved in trying to be a big group instead of like these separate groups. (Asian)

As this senior surveys her experience in Christ in Action, she feels she missed the opportunity to develop closer friendships with people from Reach. In her opinion, separate groups made it more difficult for people in Reach and in the traditional group to get to know one another. She appreciates the strength of the organization as a separate group, but still she believes it would be better for people from Reach to integrate with the larger Christ in Action group. Hence, she is suggesting that the benefits of integration experienced by members of the traditional group outweigh the benefits of separation that accrue to Reach members.

Other students who partially support race-specific groups explained that they believe these groups are beneficial to the extent that they are more successful at attracting non-Christians than are diverse groups. The primary purpose of race-specific groups should be for evangelism, these students say; otherwise, Christian organizations should strive toward diversity. As one student explains:

I think ethnic churches are good . . . even our ethnic breaking up in Christ in Action, I think it's good for the first stages of nonbelievers. But I think there has to be this goal of plugging into the greater community at large and being united as one body in Christ with those racial barriers and those socioeconomic barriers torn down because Christ destroyed the wall of hostility that separates us from them. . . . I feel really strongly that the end pursuit has to be unity and transcending those things. Those can be tolerated in the beginning especially if they help advance the gospel, but it can't stop there. (White)

Therefore, the primary goal for Christians should be unity in Christ. Unity demands racial diversity. Race- or ethnic-specific groups should only be a temporary solution for attracting non-Christians.

Another student also believes that racial separation—and Reach in particular—is good if it serves to attract non-Christians:

> I think having Reach as a separate movement is a real benefit in some ways, but yet it takes away from a bit of the diversity. I know that by having it as a separate movement, [people in Reach] have really been able to grow and flourish. It's a really strong movement. I don't know if it would establish or attract as many African American students if it were a part of Christ in Action because of the nature of how things are run, and just comfort level within your own ethnicity. . . . I know some schools have a separate Asian Christ in Action [group]. That's something I definitely would not like to see. I'd like to just maintain that cohesiveness that we have now. I think it's a great benefit to have that overlap of ethnicities. But I'm without doubt that creating separate movements does encourage certain other people to be more apt to come to the meetings and stuff. (Asian)

Like the woman above, this student recognizes that having a separate group in Christ in Action for African American students has been good. He suspects that fewer African American students would join Christ in Action if there were not a separate group. Furthermore, he implies that African American students may not be comfortable in the larger Christ in Action group. However, this same argument does not apply to Asian students. Although he can see the benefits of a race-specific group for African American students, he is not in favor of a separate group for Asian students. In his experience, the traditional Christ in Action group is unified. However, this student also regularly attends the predominantly Asian church with other Asian Christ in Action students and is a part of the close Asian friendship network within the group. Thus, although he is strongly against a separate group for Asians, his need for intraracial friendship is met through his ties within a racially homogeneous organization and social networks.

About a quarter of the students we interviewed do not support race-specific groups. Consistent with their religious reasons for racial diversity, these students believe Christians should aim to be united across race. However, white students were the most explicit and direct about their opposition.

There are definitely some ethnicities that aren't represented at large group because, I don't know if you knew but Reach, [which] is African American, [is] with Christ in Action. I don't know if I like this or not, [catering] more to them. They have a different [group]. . . . They don't really come to our large group. They could, it's not like it's at the same time [as their small group Bible studies]. They just don't go. (White)

I personally don't like the fact that [African Americans] are an entire other [group]. But if that works better for them then that's fine. I think it's sort of divisive, but maybe it's not. . . . At other schools there's an Asian part of Christ in Action too. But that's just not needed here. I think we've done a good job of diversity and making people feel comfortable. (White)

These white students are not only opposed to Reach, but see it as divisive and providing African Americans with special treatment. Further, they suggest that the limited integration between Reach and Christ in Action students is due to a lack of interest among African American students, not a lack of inclusiveness on the part of students in Christ in Action. The success of Asian integration into Christ in Action is presented as evidence. There is no need for an Asian-specific group on South Urban's campus and Asians are comfortable in Christ in Action. In so many words, Asians are again the model minority. However, this is a convenient excuse for Christ in Action students' inability to attract African Americans. As discussed earlier, white students are troubled by the tight relationships among Asians within Christ in Action.

Close to a quarter (seven) of the thirty students we interviewed are in favor of African Americans having a separate Christ in Action group. Two of these students are Asian. Not surprisingly, the strongest supporters of Reach are the six members of Reach with whom we spoke. One African American man, when asked if he believed having the Reach group separate from the traditional Christ in Action group was a good idea, replied:

I don't think Reach and Christ in Action can exist as one. I think it's good that there is a separation, but it's not like a bad separation. It's not like segregation, where people feel like "Oh, they're black" or "Oh, they're minorities." I think being a minority here on campus, you see different stuff, you go through different situations, so I think it's good to fellowship with other people who are going through some of the same things. (African American)

Another African American student agreed:

Oh yeah. Definitely. I definitely think it's good. I think it's good just to be able to find someone that you can go to and relate to. And any Christian, of course, should definitely be able to go to any Christian, but like I think it's good—geez, I don't know how to put this—it's just like the feeling of when you go home, it's like "Oh, I'm with family, I can be myself, because I'm used to this environment." So like your own comfort zone is good to come back to. And definitely you should step out of it sometimes or whatever, but it's just good to go back to that feeling of comfort and "Oh, there's somebody who can relate to me" and stuff like that. (African American)

These responses are typical of the other African American students. They reveal that African American students find refuge in Reach. In this context, they find people who understand them, who can relate to their specific situations as African American students, and who give them the freedom to be themselves. They do not expect Christ in Action to address their specific needs, preferences, or concerns. However, despite their overwhelming support for Reach, most are in favor of racial integration. Contrary to Christ in Action students, most recommend that integration with Christ in Action (as well as other Christian groups on campus) take place during extracurricular activities such as prayer meetings or social events.

Learning from This Case

This case differs from the others we've examined in two ways. First, we discuss racial diversity within a Christian organization on a secular college campus. We learn about the experiences, ideas, and social relationships of young adults. Second, we examine the place of race-specific Christian campus groups and the importance of other racially homogeneous religious organizations for people who attend an interracial group. We have found that these organizations prove to be important for building close friendships among students, particularly for racial minorities.

However, we have also found that racial homogeneity can pose a threat to within-group unity.

In Christ in Action, race-specific subgroups are particularly important for racial minorities. Reach, for example, is vital to the social and religious lives of African American students on South Urban University's campus. It facilitates their transition to college life and serves as their surrogate family. The students in Reach have a very close, dense friendship network and rely upon one another for support, acceptance, and direction in a foreign environment. All of the students recognize Reach as a very important part of their lives. Although they support racial diversity within the church, they would not sacrifice what they have in Reach for it. They would rather reserve racial integration for activities that are peripheral to the organization. In many ways, Reach provides the kind of ethnic support and cultural outlet that the Latino Sunday School provides the Latino attenders at Wilcrest. Students have a social space that is their own. They can practice their specific cultural preferences and also benefit from being a part of the larger student organization.

Furthermore, among some of the Asian students in this study, the Greater Metro Asian Church (GMAC), a predominantly Asian church, is a very important source for friendship and connectedness. These students' closest friends attend both GMAC and Christ in Action. For at least one student, GMAC was the more important of these two organizations for building a close social network. Therefore, although these students are active participants in an interracial campus organization, they draw upon their ties to a predominantly Asian church for support and friendship.

For both of these groups, racially distinct religious organizations are important to the quality of their Christian college experience. Compared to white students, both groups are more satisfied with their experience in Christ in Action. Moreover, they continue to place a high value on racial diversity. Although we do not have direct evidence that Asian students' connections to GMAC and African American students' connections to Reach give them the freedom to participate actively in racially diverse settings or to pursue opportunities for racial diversity, we can infer, based upon previous research on intergroup organizations,[1] that these organizations at least make racial integration less of a threat to their sense of identity and social connection and likely encourage them to further pursue interracial interaction.

However, race-specific subgroups are a concern for whites, and to some degree for Asians as well. White students express the greatest opposition or uneasiness with the Asian presence in Christ in Action and with Reach. White students feel that the Asian friendship group is exclusive. They also feel that the large proportion of Asians in the group is a hindrance to potential newcomers who are not Asian. Yet, interestingly, given that the group is equally white, these white students do not perceive the large white presence at Christ in Action as a hindrance to potential newcomers. Additionally, Reach is seen as divisive. Having a separate group for African American students is, to some extent, seen as a form of inequality because African Americans are receiving special treatment. Moreover, white students in Christ in Action place the burden of racial integration on Reach students. Asian students are presented as an example of how successful Christ in Action is at including racial minorities.

Second to African Americans themselves, Asians were the most supportive of Reach. However, some Asian respondents were not particularly supportive of the tight bonds among certain Asians within Christ in Action. Like the white students, some Asian students think that the Asian friendship group is exclusive and inappropriate in a racially diverse organization. Another reason given is that homogeneous friendship groups, of any kind, are not functional among Christians because they limit the group's capacity to evangelize non-Christians. The opposite reasoning is given in support of Reach, however. The homogeneity of the group is good for attracting non-Christian African Americans.

Racially homogeneous groups within interracial organizations are both beneficial and costly. For those who are in the group, it is a wonderful source of connection and support. People are more satisfied with their interracial experience if they have a homogeneous group to act as a support. Therefore, they are supportive of creating more ways to develop or improve racial diversity. However, for people who are not a part of the homogeneous group, racial homogeneity within interracial organizations can be a source of uneasiness and discomfort. It can even be threatening. In this regard, racial homogeneity can weaken the unity within an interracial organization.

Overall this case is consistent with others we have seen in that it demonstrates the importance of friendship networks in interracial religious organizations. Along with Brookside and Wilcrest, it suggests the importance of opportunities to connect with same-race groupings of people within a diverse religious organization. Like all of the other cases, it also highlights the higher expectations among white members, compared to other groups, that their interests will be reflected in the organization, and the greater level of threat felt by whites when other groups gain prominence in number and in density of same-race friendship networks. This case is important, therefore, because it shows that these relational dynamics exist in religious organizations that are not churches.

7

Jesus Is Color-Blind

A visit to the campus of Emmanuel Bible College (EBC) on the West Coast is a pleasant experience. Large trees and immaculately manicured lawns wrap the campus in a feeling of calm serenity. Smiling young clean-cut students say "hi" as they walk past you, and groups of friends sit and laugh or pray together on the grassy lawns in the courtyard. Also noticeable is that it is relatively racially diverse, at least in comparison to other private evangelical colleges. Approximately a quarter of the undergraduate population here are students of color—Asian and Hispanics account for roughly equal percentages (around 10 percent), with African American students less prevalent at around 5 percent. There is no visible tension between these groups, and indeed if one were to ask most white students and faculty here they would say that "everyone gets along well." "Perhaps there may be isolated incidents of racial insensitivity," they might add, "but there is love and acceptance here for anyone, regardless of skin color."

This picture of racial harmony begins to fade if one takes a longer walk around campus, looking more closely. One sees that the people walking around campus in what seem to be the unofficial uniforms for administrators (ties and dark suits) and faculty (khaki Dockers, blue cotton button down shirts, and brown shoes) are, with few exceptions, white males. Campus staff members who are not white are mostly janitors, groundskeepers, clerical or cafeteria workers. Pictures on display in the chapel and in some of the academic buildings portray Jesus as a European-looking man. Walking into the cafeteria during lunchtime, one sees certain tables that are filled with black students only, a few more with mostly Asian students, a few with mainly Latino students, and the large remainder with white students only. Occasionally white students will ask why other ethnic groups "segregate themselves" in the cafeteria, in ethnic clubs, or at certain spots on campus. Yet nobody seems to ask why the white kids segregate themselves as well.

These patterns would be noticeable on most predominantly white college campuses around America. With the exception of historically black universities, on most college campuses in the United States cafeteria tables are segregated, professors and administrators are disproportionately white, and low-wage service workers are disproportionately people of color. What seems different about EBC, what becomes more noticeable the longer you are there, is that there is very little dialogue about racial issues, at least in public. In fact it seems that people are unaware that these issues exist, or are possibly trying to pretend that they do not. There are no student groups protesting the lack of ethnic studies courses, there are no faculty presentations about racial issues, there are no editorials in the school newspaper about racism. On rare occasions, a white student will publish an article condemning affirmative action, but other than that, the public silence on racial issues here is deafening.

The exception to this silence is on the campus electronic bulletin board system. Similar to chat rooms, these bulletin boards allow for electronic discussions on a number of issues. The bulletin board titled "multiculturalism" is dominated by a small number of white students who think that affirmative action, diversity programs, and multiculturalism are un-American and un-Christian. Any student who disagrees with this dominant position receives a large number of critical responses immediately, often cast in angry tones and full of invective. So the one place on campus where racial issues are discussed frequently and openly is often a hostile environment for students of color.

In private conversations among students of color, the topics of race and racism on campus is never far from the surface. For many students of color, life at EBC has been painful. Like many students who enroll in distinctively evangelical colleges, most of these students came to EBC not primarily to gain professional skills, but to immerse themselves in a Christian environment, where their faith could be built up, and where they could connect with other students who share the same values and life goals. Many of these students of color, however, say that they have received more acceptance in the secular world than at EBC.

Although many of the difficulties these students of color face here may also exist on most other predominantly white college campuses, it seems that the strong white evangelical subculture at EBC produces unique racial dynamics that make the experiences of students of color particularly difficult. These dynamics are the focus of this chapter.

Diversity at EBC in Historical Context

EBC was founded in the 1920s as a Bible college offering two-year courses in a "practical working knowledge" of the Bible and in evangelistic techniques. This nondenominational college was one of a number of Bible institutes, Bible colleges, and evangelical liberal arts colleges that were important in the emergence and development of the fundamentalist movement in the first half of the twentieth century. The basic function of these schools was to provide an alternative to denominational seminaries and colleges that were seen by many conservative Protestants as being too influenced by secular naturalism and humanism. These schools thus became important in unifying the various strands of fundamentalism, in socializing new generations of young people into fundamentalist values, and in creating an institutional bulwark against secular modernism (Flory 1997).

In the first half of the twentieth century, EBC primarily trained pastors and lay church members in doctrine and evangelistic techniques. With the expansion of higher education in America after World War II, EBC and many of the other Bible colleges and institutes became accredited four-year liberal arts colleges, and they expanded their offerings to include bachelor's degrees in a number of academic disciplines.

EBC currently attracts students who want to combine training in biblical theology with a degree program in a particular discipline. EBC now offers bachelor's degrees in more than twenty majors. The primary selling points for EBC are that each academic discipline, from art to business to nursing, is taught from within a "biblical worldview" and each student receives training in biblical interpretation from professional theologians. EBC recruits mostly from conservative evangelical churches and private Christian schools in the region.

Throughout its history, the EBC student body has been predominantly white. Table 7.1 shows the virtual absence of students of color at EBC until the 1980s.

This absence of non-white students can be attributed to two main factors. First, racial segregation among conservative Protestant denominations, such as the Baptists, meant that theologically conservative African American churches and denominations had their own educational institutions to train pastors. Second, the agenda from which Bible colleges such as EBC sprang—primarily the fundamentalist-modernist debate— was not particularly salient for African American Protestants. In addi-

TABLE 7.I
EBC Enrollment by Ethnicity, Various Years

Year	Asian	Black	Hispanic	White	International	Other	Total
1927	2%	0	0	98	–	–	329
1930	3	0	1	96	–	–	215
1938	2	0	0	98	–	–	319
1940	1	0	2	97	–	–	406
1945	1	0	1	98	–	–	739
1950	3	1	0	96	–	–	772
1955	2	1	2	95	–	–	671
1960	3	2	2	93	–	–	710
1965	2	0	0	98	–	–	926
1970	2	2	0	96	–	–	657
1976	2	1	2	93	2	–	2066
1980	3	2	3	89	3		2193
1985	6	3	2	85	3	1	1891
1995	13	5	7	67	6		2051
2002	9	4	8	74	4	–	2841

SOURCE: Flory 1997

tion, the rapid growth in numbers of evangelical Latinos and Asians did not begin until the 1970s.

The more liberal Protestant denominations and seminaries were much more open to progressive thinking in the area of civil rights, which was a more important issue for African American Protestants. In addition, many Bible colleges in the south were officially segregated institutions in the early twentieth century. Thus, many African Americans looking for religious instruction chose mainstream Protestant or specifically African American institutions. There seems to have been little incentive for African Americans to attend a college like EBC.

Likewise, there were few Hispanic churches and institutions engaged in the fundamentalist-modernist debate in the early 1900s. The rapid growth of the evangelical movement in Latin American countries and Chicano communities did not begin until the 1970s. Hispanic evangelicalism has also tended to have a more Pentecostal rather than fundamentalist flavor. EBC throughout its history has been cool at some times, and outwardly hostile at others, to Pentecostal theology. EBC has historically drawn more from Asian American communities, particularly Korean American, as well as from Asia, where evangelical Protestantism took hold in the twentieth century. In Korea, EBC has a good reputation among conservative evangelical churches as a place where students can get good Bible training, untainted by liberal interpretations of Scripture. EBC continues to have significant numbers of Korean students, both from

Korea and from the United States. Still, compared to white students, their numbers are relatively small.

Throughout the 1980s the school gradually became more diverse, until it reached its current level of diversity in the mid-1990s. Most of these students of color were Asian, Hispanic, and international students; the school continued to have a low percentage of African Americans. The growth in diversity since the 1980s is probably due primarily to the ethnic transformation of the west coast during that period and to the increasing numbers of evangelicals among Asian and Hispanic communities. The college during that period of increasing diversity also made some institutional efforts to recruit students of color and provide special scholarships for students of color in financial need, which probably had an impact as well. An office of multicultural programs was also formed around this time, and it facilitated the organization of ethnic clubs on campus and an entry program to help students of color adjust to the environment on the campus. Despite its strong white majority, EBC is roughly as diverse as the average private college nationwide, and is much more diverse than most other private evangelical colleges (see table 7.2). It thus provides an interesting case study of an evangelical college that has been somewhat successful in attracting a diverse student body.

Despite the university's modest success in attracting a fairly diverse student body, university records show that black and Hispanic students at EBC have lower retention rates than do white and Asian students. Asian students actually have the highest retention rate, followed by whites, then Hispanics and black students, in that order. There may be a number of reasons for these lower retention rates among black and Hispanic students. One could be that as a private college, EBC does not offer much in the way of scholarships for under-represented students, which may make the school too expensive for minority students who can find greater opportunities for financial aid at other colleges. We believe that the campus racial climate has something to do with it as well.

An understanding of the current racial dynamics at EBC requires some understanding of its history. First, the school holds the Bible to be the source of absolute truth, in matters of living the Christian life as well as in matters of nature, culture, and history. Second, the culture of the school tends to promote a suspicion of secular academic practices and institutions. This tension with secular academia sometimes gets translated into opposition to any ideas or social reforms that are seen as being "secular" or "liberal." Since the advancement of civil rights for minority

TABLE 7.2
Percentage of Undergraduate Enrollment by Ethnicity, 2000

	EBC	All U.S. Evangelical Colleges	All U.S. Private Colleges
%White	75	88	73
%African American	5	6	12
%Hispanic	10	4	6
%Asian	10	2	9

NOTES: Excludes international students.
SOURCE: National Association for Education Statistics

groups is often seen by white evangelicals as part of "secular liberalism" there has been suspicion of this agenda. Finally, the theology that is promoted by this and other Bible colleges arising out of fundamentalism has always been focused on the individual rather than on the reform of social institutions. This individualistic tendency comes partially from a theology known as pre-millennialism, advocated by many conservative evangelicals. According to this doctrine, the social world will decline and become more and more corrupt until Jesus returns to set up his eternal kingdom. Thus, while reforming the world before that time may be well-intended, time is more effectively spent focusing on evangelism and preparing individuals for Christ's return. These aspects of the college's subculture have an enormous impact on the way race and ethnicity are understood and experienced at this campus.

Unfulfilled Expectations

Many students of color expressed in their interviews that they came to EBC with high expectations for their college experience. Most of these students came to EBC for the same reasons that white students were there: to get an education that would strengthen their understanding of the Christian faith and to be in an environment where they would be surrounded by fellow Christians who would embrace them and support their resolve to live the Christian life. For many of these students of color, these expectations were only partially fulfilled. Most of them expressed that they had learned much that was beneficial for their life and their faith, and that they had made close friendships, mostly with other students of color. Most, however, also spoke at length of how disappointing their experiences at EBC have been.

Most of these students of color recounted numerous difficult and painful experiences during their time at EBC. By far the most frequently mentioned difficulty was enduring offensive and ignorant remarks by white students about racial topics. Most of these comments seem to spring from a lack of exposure to diversity and from deeply held conservative social and political beliefs. Immigration is a particularly heated topic, as this region on the west coast has been dramatically transformed by immigration in the last two decades. When immigration issues are discussed in class, students of color are often the only ones taking a pro-immigration stance. And when white students make ignorant or offensive statements, students of color complain that professors rarely intervene in the discussion. As one Latino student told us:

> I had a class where they were teaching about poverty and [a student] made a comment about how Latinos [are] lazy. The teacher didn't stop them and I'm thinking, "Why doesn't the teacher stop them?" I don't get it. Like they didn't hear it or something. And then other people get offended but the teachers don't say anything. Then when you stand up you feel like this little person talking to a bunch of people who don't understand you. And even if you talk to them, they probably won't get it. I think [teachers] should be standing up for you.

This sense of feeling alone in a hostile crowd, with no support from the faculty, was a common theme in many interviews. Many simply try to detach from the class discussions as a result.

> I get to a point where I just don't say anything anymore. When the whole class is going off on you, you feel like you're just one small person, so it's not worth it. People say nasty things about immigrants and immigration in class a lot. I start getting emotional, so I choose not to get involved. I like to debate things rationally, not emotionally, so I can't get involved in that. (Latino student)

Other examples of offensive statements by white students recalled by students of color include "we should just nuke the Chinese," "Indians should be forced to live on reservations," "Whites are smarter than other groups," and "you have Black history month, why do you need a club?" Having to endure offensive and ignorant comments from white students is a common complaint from students of color at other predominantly white colleges (Hurtado et al. 1999). However, some students of color we interviewed who had gone to predominantly white public high schools said that these comments were more frequent at EBC than at their high schools because of the average EBC student's relative lack of exposure to diversity.

I came from a predominantly white high school but it was a public high school and I never dealt with any of this until I came to EBC. I think it's because—I hate to say to this—but a lot of Christians are narrow-minded and they grow up in their little churches with the same people and don't step out of their comfort zone. . . . It's not fair for their parents to raise them like that. Their parents grew up in a sheltered, very closed environment where everything around them is [seen as] wrong. They were just taught that way because they were so sheltered growing up but they know nothing else. A lot of them are home-schooled that come to EBC, and a lot of them are from small, Christian schools, and they don't have experience in the real world. (Latino student)

This sentiment was one we heard often from students of color, and it is supported by admissions data. Around a third of the undergraduate student body at EBC were home-schooled or attended conservative Christian private schools, which are predominantly white. Thus, a significant minority of white undergraduates here probably did not have much contact with students of color in high school and many were probably not exposed to much information about the experiences of different ethnic groups in America.

Another problem students of color expressed repeatedly was the difficulty of fitting in socially with the white majority. They reported that while most white students were polite to them, this politeness did not extend to welcoming them into white social circles.

In interactions with people on campus, if you're not with your friends, nobody talks to you. You feel invisible. Nobody says "hi." I talked to a white student about this once and she said, "If you're not in my realm, I probably won't notice you." It was like people feel you are different so they don't want to talk to you. (African American student)

This sense of feeling invisible and not being accepted into white social circles seems to be common among students of color at all predominantly white colleges, whether religious or not (Hurtado et al. 1999). What seems particularly painful for students of color, however, is that they had such high expectations of being accepted and supported at a Christian college.

> It may not be worse than other places, but what makes it worse is that you expect that a Christian place would be better than the rest of the world. A lot of us are the only Christians in our families or in our friends, so we wanted to come here to be embraced and built up. So it's an even bigger letdown when it's not like that. (African American student)

Interestingly, building close friendships quickly and easily was almost unanimously cited as the aspect of EBC our white interviewees enjoyed the most. In fact, most of the white students we interviewed expressed the belief that minority students probably have a much better experience at EBC than they would at secular colleges because the people are so welcoming and embracing here.

> Interviewer: What are the things that you have enjoyed most about being at EBC?
> White student: The dorm life. I live in [dorm name], so it's all girls. We do lots of activities, I love the RAs, and I have really close friendships with the girls on my floor. So just seeing how everyone connects so easily is great.
> Interviewer: Do you think it's difficult for minority students to be at EBC?
> White student: No, not at all. Everyone treats everyone the same on the same level. I think it would be much easier for them here than it would be at a public school because everyone is so accepting here.

This white student's impression is the opposite of what most students of color reported. Many students of color at EBC described being in a state of shock their first year at EBC. After choosing a Christian college over secular colleges, many of which had offered lucrative financial packages, because they wanted to live and learn in a supportive Christian environment, they found the mismatch between expectations and reality extremely painful. A Filipina student expressed the shock she felt in her first week of orientation her freshman year:

I initially went in really positive—I'm going to make friends and get involved, and I assumed people would be open to you. I assumed people would be loving. It all started [orientation] week. Everyone's meeting each other and I was really enthusiastic. One day we went to a baseball game. We were on the bus with my friend. Everyone around us was introducing themselves to each other and meeting each other, but wouldn't say anything to us. There were people on the bus in front of us and people in back of us, and they were introducing themselves to each other over our heads, but they wouldn't look at us. At the game nobody talked to us at all. I felt really isolated. I still hate baseball now because of that [laughs].

On the way home, the same thing happened. Everyone was talking around us and over us, but it was like we were invisible. I talked to [another Filipina] and asked her if that ever happened to her and she said yes and so we talked about it and the same things were happening to her and she was having a really hard time. We cried together about it. We had this mixed friend [half white, half Filipina] who looks more white, and she didn't have the same things happen to her.

We talked to another Filipino friend about it and he said "This is just how it is. You can't change it, so just get used to it." We were so mad. We were saying "We're Christians, we're supposed to stand up for what is right." (Filipina student)

Some students of color never get over this shock and leave the school embittered. Others who stay find solace with other students of color dealing with the same sense of isolation. For some, these relationships with other students of color have been the reason they have stayed and the most positive aspect of being at EBC.

Divided by Faith

Another painful aspect of life for many students of color at EBC is having their faith questioned (by other students) because their ways of thinking about the Christian life and living it out differ from the white majority. Because the majority of students come from conservative white families and churches, their way of expressing and living out their faith differs significantly from that of people who have grown up in other communities.

Interviewer: What were the hardest things about being at EBC?

Korean American former student: Feeling that people had this idea of what "spiritual" is, and people looking at me as if I was less spiritual because I didn't fit that idea.

This sense of being judged negatively for not fitting in with the white majority's view of the Christian life came up repeatedly in our interviews. Some also said that these types of challenges eventually led them to question their own faith, and whether they were really believers.

People just think what they grew up with and assume it's biblical. But it's so the opposite of what I grew up with. Sometimes I have to remind myself that I'm still a Christian and have a close relationship with God even though I don't think like people here do. You get to the point where you start questioning yourself, whether you're really a Christian because people can't believe some of the things I say. People forget about all of the aspects of God's character here. People are self-righteous. They think what they believe is biblical and if you don't think like they do they say, "You are so liberal." And they use the word "liberal" like it's an insult. (Latino student)

The faith of the white majority at EBC appears to be highly individualistic, which tends to be a key feature of white evangelicalism (Emerson and Smith 2000). Students are encouraged to have daily "quiet times" where they separate themselves from others to pray and study the Bible by themselves. They are also encouraged to live personally holy lives in obedience to the commands of Scripture. While these themes are consistent with historic Protestantism, the corporate aspects of the faith— building a community of love, care for the hurting, and social justice— seem to be under-emphasized here. These are typically the themes that are more emphasized in African American, Hispanic, and to a lesser extent Asian Protestant churches. This emphasis on the individual rather than the community seems to be at the center of the conflict between white and minority conceptions of the Christian life at EBC.

Interviewer: You talk about the Christian subculture at EBC. Could you define that subculture and talk about how it affects people?

African American student: It's individualistic and heavily works driven. You have to have your quiet time every day and pray a certain way. Validity is placed only on head knowledge, not heart or experience. Even in music, only one type is accepted. Anything outside of that narrow road and your salvation gets questioned. I know how God changed my family. We're changed completely. At EBC, my faith was questioned because it wasn't part of the mold. I started questioning whether I was a Christian because my faith does not look like theirs, my church does not look like theirs. (African American student)

As this student expressed, the dominant emphasis on Bible knowledge or "head knowledge" was a key difference from the "heart-" or "experience-based" faith that many students of color grew up with. An African American student, writing an editorial in the school newspaper her senior year, profoundly articulated this difference.

The God I serve is not the one you have depicted to me. You present Him as able to be grasped intellectually. His existence is proven through a series of logical arguments. My mother only gave me one argument— He is. That was all I needed to know. I learned that because He is, I can face tomorrow and life is worth living just because He is. Perhaps this is not enough for you, but I need more than a logical series of arguments to see me through my trials. I would not have survived the struggles God has put me through if in the midst of them I was still trying to prove His existence to myself. . . . You focus on understanding God, dissecting Him and putting Him back together and then applying Him like decorative wallpaper to your life. I have been taught to experience Him every day. He is the air that I breathe, my very sustenance for life.

According to many of the students of color we interviewed, this emphasis on knowledge rather than experience tends to produce arrogance in those who possess more of that knowledge, and that translates into a contentious environment.

The sinful superiority that you see here is just wrong. Holding up intelligence—if you can exegete Scripture, you're valued. If not, you're seen as less, or you aren't seen as someone worth listening to. They miss out on other characteristics of God that can bless them because they don't listen. I was able to learn from them, but they miss out on that learning. (African American student)

It seems that the individualistic and knowledge-based faith that is promoted at EBC would be fine with many of the students of color we interviewed if it were acknowledged that it is but one way to look at the Christian life, and if white students were interested in learning about their traditions in return. The fact that the culturally specific way of viewing and living the Christian life is portrayed as the only way to live it out is what causes frustration. Many students of color expressed thankfulness that they had expanded their knowledge and view of the faith through their encounters with this white evangelical subculture. Most, surprisingly, said that if they had to do it over again, they would choose again to attend EBC because of this. But they also expressed hurt that their unique cultural insights, which could help white students understand the faith more fully, were not valued. The same African American student quoted above in the school newspaper expressed in that article disappointment in white students' lack of interest in her culture:

> I expected you to be interested in who I am, what I am like, how I grew up, where I come from. I expected you to care, but you didn't. When I asked to set aside time in which I could share with you aspects of who I am, you complained. When the cafeteria served my food, you complained. When someone delivered a [sermon] or sang a song in my language, you complained. When I put much effort into planning and presenting events whereby you could learn more about me, you didn't come.

All of this seems to suggest that at least among the white students at EBC, there is a majority view of how the Christian life is to be expressed and lived out, and that anything that does not conform to that view is disregarded—or condemned. The lack of willingness to explore other ways of experiencing the faith, ways in which other cultures express Christian truth, seems to be due to a combination of factors that are discussed in the next section.

God Is Color-Blind

If you ask white students and faculty at EBC how the various ethnic groups on campus get along, they will say "by and large, very well." Most seem completely unaware of the difficulties we describe in the preceding sections of this chapter. This lack of awareness is typical among majority groups as a result of their structural position in the majority (Tatum 1997). The lack of awareness seems to be exacerbated at EBC by the suppression of dialogue about racial issues on campus.

Students of color in our interviews repeatedly mentioned the backlash they experienced from white students when they spoke out about the difficulties of EBC life for students of color. This backlash is couched in religious terms—that talking about racial issues and cultural differences produces disunity in the "body of Christ."

Relational harmony seems to be a high value at this college, in which is consistent with the findings of other studies of white evangelicalism (Emerson and Smith 2000). For most white students and faculty on campus, the key to relational harmony between racial groups is to see each other as individuals rather than as part of a group. As a result, talking about racial issues is seen to undermine this unity because by definition talk about race is talk about groups rather than individuals. Harmony, therefore, is produced by individuals becoming color-blind. This color-blind ideal is dominant among white Americans, regardless of religious preference (Bonilla-Silva 2001; Wellman 1977). But the promotion of this ideal seems more intense at EBC because of the importance placed on the unity of believers.

According to one student:

> For EBC students race is an afterthought. They have this idea that love is color-blind, Jesus is color-blind, color-blind is the ideal—don't see someone's race or background. So it produces this attitude of let's be closed off to differences, differences cause conflict and affect our unity. The hardest part about it is that it produces a culture that's very invalidating to pain. If [white students] don't want to talk about [racial issues], then it's you that's the problem for bringing it up. Your pain is overlooked and invalidated. You're the one who sticks out so it's you that's the problem. It makes you question yourself. Why can't you just get along or do things their way and be OK with it? The fortress mentality makes people not want to talk about it. (Chinese American student)

The color-blind ideal seems to put students of color in a no-win situation. White students, in their ignorance, often make comments or public statements that are offensive and hurtful. If students of color express their hurt or try to explain why the comment was offensive, they are criticized for being divisive, with the implication that they are being "un-Christian" for bringing up racial issues. This is particularly painful and aggravating to the students of color because merely for expressing their views, they wind up not only having their emotions invalidated, but also, again, having their faith called into question.

This double bind is illustrated in an incident that happened on campus. As a joke, a poster was put up on campus that had a degrading image of a person of color. This poster offended a number of minority students. It was not intended to offend, but there was a great deal of hurt and anger. A debate ensued on the campus bulletin board about the appropriateness of the poster. One white student offered this attempt at defusing the situation:

> I can understand why you would find offense in this joke but I think you are looking at it from the wrong perspective and I am so sorry it has caused you and others such anguish. I guarantee it was not done in malice or with any demeaning intentions, but only as a comic relief if you will. I also am curious why such an uproar is needed over the matter? I hope that this letter has helped you to understand the intent of this poster and enabled you to let go of your anger.

This response is instructive. It reveals a number of assumptions prevalent among the white majority here that make dialogue over racial issues extremely difficult. First, the author of this note assumes that the important issue at hand was the intention of the person who put up the poster. If the person did not intend to offend anyone, then there should be no problem, and if one has a problem with it, they have *the wrong perspective*. This reveals a strong individualism—the intention or the "heart" of the individual is all that matters, not larger community dynamics that serve to create division despite the intentions of individuals. If one departs from this individualist ethic, one is seen as being divisive or sinfully stuck in one's anger. Since the student of color is seen as being in the wrong for expressing anger, the result is the suppression of dialogue about race.

The transition from differences in perception to matters of right and wrong seems to happen quickly in this environment, given the high value placed on absolutes of right and wrong in every aspect of life at EBC. The majority view often gets defined as the "right" or "moral" view. The author of the above note sees the main issue to be addressed is getting the objecting person to "let go of their anger" rather than understanding the root of the objection—why posters like this are offensive.

"Unity" among believers is defined as good relations between individuals, but these individuals are not seen as parts of a larger social context.

Thus, larger social structural issues that cause divisions among believers are ignored, and the solutions for disharmony lie with the individual—the individual must let go of anger, forgive, and get back into a right relationship. This leaves the larger social structures and norms unexamined and therefore places the burden of unity on the offended minority group. As a result, well-intentioned responses like the one above only serve to exacerbate the divide between students.

Another white student was more blunt in assessing the debate over the derogatory posters:

> The poster was never meant to be racist. If you found that it was racist then I feel sorry for you when you get out in the real world because it's just going to get a whole lot worse for you then. If you want to say that it could have been a little disrespectful because of the person they chose then I could lean towards your side but that's not the case for most people that are posting here. They are saying that it's a racist poster. The only reason that there is still racism in the world today is because people want it to be. They want something to make them feel good. When there's an issue they find racism in it and get all blown up over it and try stirring things up.

This is a common perception among white people in America—that racism exists only in the minds of minorities, and divisions come from their "stirring things up" by crying racism over misperceptions. Within the evangelical subculture this view is often given religious backing by promoting a color-blind theology—that God cares about us as individuals and that our identity is "in Christ" rather than in our ethnicity. Thus, talking about race and emphasizing our ethnicity only causes divisions, and we should therefore focus on what we have in common, our faith, and not what makes us different. This view effectively silences dialogue about race on campus and assumes that the faith lived by the majority white population is the faith that is common to all. As a result, the expression "Let's focus on what we have in common" effectively places the burden of conformity to this subculture on students of color.

Political Correctness, Multiculturalism, and Other Evils

Another obstacle to racial dialogue the white evangelical subculture seems to create on this campus is the idea that promoting diversity and emphasizing ethnic differences is part of a wider multicultural movement that is relativistic and godless at its core. Since the biblical passages that promote justice and reconciliation between ethnic groups are not emphasized at EBC, it is often assumed that the Bible is not centrally concerned with ethnic and racial issues. Since the individual's relationship with God is given ultimate importance in this subculture, cultural differences in how people think about and live out their faith do not seem to be emphasized, and an understanding of ethnicity and culture is not emphasized as being relevant to advancing an understanding of Christian life. As a result, emphasizing diversity and multiculturalism is seen by many only as a "liberal political agenda" that has nothing to do with their faith.

An institutional audit was conducted recently at EBC to assess how students of color experience life on campus. The motivation behind this study was fourfold. First, there is concern that if EBC does not do a better job recruiting and retaining students of color, the college will not be able to survive in an increasingly non-white region. Second, the college holds the "great commission" to "make disciples of all nations" in very high regard. This college is a training ground for many overseas evangelical missionaries and therefore is outward-looking in its faith. The importance of sharing the good news of Jesus with the world is central to EBC's mission statement. It is understood that EBC needs to be able to train leaders from all different types of communities so that they can then effectively take the good news to those communities. Third, the college is accredited by a regional body for which diversity is a high priority. To be accredited by this body, the institution must show that it is able to serve and effectively educate a diverse student population. Finally, some administrators were sincerely concerned about reports they had heard of negative experiences faced by students of color.

This institutional audit was publicized in the EBC alumni newsletter and around campus. While many reactions to the commissioning of the study were very positive, a significant number of students and alumni reacted negatively. Here is a sampling of negative e-mails and posts on the campus bulletin board system in response to announcement of the study.

> EBC's "landmark study on ethnic and cultural diversity" mentioned in the latest [newsletter] is immoral. Furthermore, it's an irresponsible waste of my tuition dollars that I entrusted the school to educate people with. (Student on electronic bulletin board)

I always thought that EBC was above all the PC racialism that infects American academia. So it really bothers me when I see them implementing the same types of programs and keeping people on staff that can't even recognize that racialism is evil. (Alumnus on electronic bulletin board)

Another e-mail sent to the principal investigator of this study by a current graduate student questions the validity of the philosophy behind the research:

Although I have not read the survey you conducted I have heard reaction by those who have read it. I am a masters student [at EBC] and would disagree with the philosophy behind this multicultural propaganda that this survey seems to be emulating. I recommend a book by professor Peter Wood entitled, "Diversity: The Invention of a Concept." This book reveals some of what is wrong with this so-called humanistic trend in the name of "diversity" that has overtaken the education community in America.

These posts are interesting because they show that talking about and promoting ethnic diversity are seen as "immoral" and "evil" at least by some students at EBC. It also shows that EBC has something of a reputation, at least in some quarters, as a place to go to get away from the "political correctness" that has "taken over" the secular universities.

The history of EBC has been to offer an alternative to the "humanism" of secular universities. Because the white evangelical church does not emphasize biblical teachings on social justice and racial reconciliation, promoting diversity seems to be seen by many as part of the secular humanist agenda.

In some quarters of this college, multiculturalism is also associated with "postmodernism," which for some white evangelicals constitutes the principal threat to Christianity in contemporary American culture. Proponents of this view often equate postmodernism with moral relativism, which according to them undermines the ability to make claims for the universal truth of the Christian faith. Multiculturalism, therefore, and talk about how culture affects what we understand to be truth are heated and contentious issues on this campus. One faculty member put it this way:

I think certain components [on campus] have created a straw man—called postmodernism—that has become a whipping boy. And postmodernism becomes this one narrowly defined thing. It's not one thing, it's many things, and it's not all bad. But it gets defined narrowly, then it gets lumped in with buzzwords like multiculturalism and pluralism, and these things begin to be seen as negative. I have students ask me sometimes, when I talk about multiculturalism or pluralism, "Isn't that postmodern?" And that is seen as evil. In [certain departments] postmodernism is seen as a heretical philosophy. As a result, we become cautious about celebrating diversity. (White faculty member)

This contentiousness further complicates efforts by students and faculty to understand the cultural differences that exist in the student population and how they relate to the Christian life.

Finding a Home

A number of students of color we interviewed at EBC told us that the best part of their experience at EBC was with the programs associated with the college's department of multiethnic programs. This is a department created in the 1980s as an effort to make the school better able to serve a diverse population. The director of this department, Mark Mori, who is an Asian American, has developed a number of programs, including retreats, alternative chapels, clubs, and courses, to provide a forum in which to discuss and process racial issues that affect the campus and the wider society. He has also promoted a theology of racial justice and reconciliation that provides a biblical framework for understanding these issues. Most participants in these programs are students of color, but a small number of white students have become involved as well.

Many of the students of color we interviewed cited these programs as the highlight of their time at EBC. In fact, some stated that had these programs not existed, they would have left EBC. According to many students, these programs provide a much-needed safe place to dialogue about racial issues and to find a community for alienated students of color.

Interviewer: What did you enjoy most about being at EBC?
Filipino student: The [multiethnic program] retreats, Mark's programs. It was a place where you could explore culture and issues,

and where you could talk freely. I was able to make close friends there. They are the friends that I still have.

African American student: I enjoyed the multiethnic programs and department that Mark is in charge of. I enjoyed Mark and all of the services that he provides. Although you feel marginalized at EBC, you can always find some other marginalized person that you can relate to. That's not to EBC's credit, because they're not trying to do that but there is always someone you can find that you can relate to. But I never felt a part of the majority community. I always felt outside of that community. But with Mark and his group, I found a home. Those are the people I still stay in touch with, along with the people in Gospel choir.

In these programs, students learn what the Bible has to say about social structures and social justice as they relate to racial issues. Students of color are often energized by this biblical knowledge that speaks to their situation of alienation at EBC and in the larger culture. Many are also discouraged by the fact that these things are not taught in their Bible classes. A Chinese American student expressed his discouragement at the disconnect between what he was learning in Mark's program and what he was hearing in his Bible classes.

Race, class, and gender issues are not talked about in Bible classes. Which is incredible because the Bible is always talking about these things. Jesus' parables are always talking about which groups are valued and who's not, and the different values of the kingdom. (Chinese American student)

The multiethnic programs at EBC are interesting because they show that a religiously based educational program need not alienate minority groups if the issues are explored openly and sensitively. In fact, these programs seem to suggest that if the basis for promoting diversity and racial reconciliation is grounded religiously, the passion and motivation to pursue these goals can increase. A professor who teaches courses in race and multicultural education confirmed this:

Since students have such a high view of the Bible, if you show them that the Bible really promotes cultural understanding and racial reconciliation, then students are all over it. (White professor)

At this college, however, there seem to be few professors that are able to make that connection between their religious faith and understanding and promoting racial justice and reconciliation. Or at least it seems that they do not make that connection publicly.

A View from the Top

Despite the obstacles to understanding and embracing diversity at EBC, all of the faculty members and administrators that we interviewed, somewhat surprisingly, expressed that promoting diversity should be a central priority for the college. Indeed, the mission statement of the university and a recently published "vision statement" to guide the university in the next ten years prioritized the need to recruit students and faculty of color and to reflect the ethnic diversity of the surrounding region.

However, EBC faculty and administrators gave interesting and differing reasons why diversity is important. These responses fall essentially into three categories. The first is the idea that we have knowledge that is important for all people to know, and diversifying will permit all ethnic groups to benefit from the knowledge we have to teach. The second is that the community of Christian believers worldwide—or "the body," as it is referred to—is very diverse, so the school should reflect that. Furthermore, it is important to learn how to live together as one body, and students should be able to see this modeled in a Christian college. This was the most common response.

> Interviewer: Do you think it's important for EBC to become more ethnically diverse?
> Faculty member: Definitely. We come here because we all want to serve God and are unified in that, but we are also diverse, so students would benefit from seeing that unity and diversity.

The third response, which came up in only a few interviews with white faculty and in no interviews with administrators, was that having faculty and students from different backgrounds and perspectives gives us a fuller understanding of the issues concerning the faith and how it relates to the various academic disciplines.

In American higher education, the most influential argument for diversity is an academic one (Musil 1999). Many now believe that diversity is deeply linked to insuring academic excellence—having multiple perspectives enhances scholarship and advances knowledge. This idea seems largely absent among faculty at EBC, and nonexistent among administrators. For the most part, it seems that diversity at EBC is desired because all people can benefit from the knowledge the institution has to offer, and because it can be an example of how Christians from different backgrounds can be unified. A lack of commitment to the idea that diversity enhances knowledge seems to produce an environment where the different perspectives of students and faculty of color are not appreciated, but rather criticized for deviating from the campus norms. This kind of environment also offers little incentive for white students and faculty to learn about and embrace other cultures and the ways in which they express their faith.

Beginnings of a Transformation?

The audit to assess the experiences of students of color was commissioned by EBC's top administrators because they were concerned about a recent trend of lower enrollment percentages and retention rates for students of color at the school. The demographic transformation of the region and the need to compete in an increasingly non-white marketplace in the future was also a factor. Administrators were also aware that a number of students of color do not have the best experiences at EBC, and the regional accrediting agency prioritizes the ability of accredited colleges to provide a quality educational experience for minority students. Some were also concerned personally about the reports of painful experiences among students of color.

At the time of this writing, the results of the audit have prompted a more public dialogue about racial and ethnic issues on campus. Many of the findings reported here were also reported in the audit. There have been a number of presentations at faculty and staff meetings concerning the painful experiences many students of color have at EBC. This has resulted in some efforts to increase representation of different racial groups in chapel, among the faculty, and in student activities. Since this initiative is in the early stages it is difficult to see what, if any, results it will yield.

There seems to be potential for structural changes toward a more inclusive campus.

Learning from This Case

This case is unique in our sample because, unlike the others, it is an educational institution. It is also much larger than the other cases and has a higher percentage of white people. Despite these differences, we see some similarities to the racial dynamics found in our other cases. Some of these dynamics may be exaggerated, however, because of the unique character of this college. We must keep in mind, for example, that this institution is on the conservative end of the theological spectrum, which may produce dynamics that do not exist in more mainstream religious colleges. It is important to recognize, however, that this organization is among the most diverse evangelical colleges in America, and despite its failings EBC has been more successful in drawing a diverse student body than many private colleges, whether secular or religious.

The most noticeable racial dynamic in this organization is religiously charged ethnocentrism. As we have observed in our other cases, people in religious groups endow cultural differences with transcendent meanings, making compromise difficult. The dominant feature of the conservative white evangelical subculture on this campus is its individualistic interpretation of the Christian faith. This college promotes a Christian worldview where the top priorities are the individual's personal relationship with God and the ability of individuals to interpret the Bible correctly. The primary struggle students of color experience at EBC is the sense that their faith is always being questioned because they do not conform to the dominant culture's way of expressing it. At this college, the majority view of how the faith should be understood and lived out is seen simply as the "biblical" norm. When differences in expressions of faith are noticed, they are seen not as rooted in culture, but as rooted in absolutes. Thus, the majority view of how the faith is to be understood is seen as the true or biblical way, and divergent views are seen as being grounded in error.

Because this is a religious educational institution, the religiously charged ethnocentrism is likely magnified as compared to other types of organizations. The main purpose of this institution is to transfer knowledge of the "true" way of living out the faith. Since there is not a diverse representation of different ethnic groups transferring that knowledge, the true way tends to be defined according to white conservative cultural interpretations.

Another effect of the individualistic culture at this college is the pervasive assumption that unity is achieved by being "color-blind" and ignoring racial and cultural differences. Emphasizing membership in a common "body," the Christian faith, rather than focusing on group identities is also seen as a key to harmony. When students of color bring up racial issues and cultural differences, they are viewed as being "divisive" and are advised to focus on what unifies rather than on things that have the potential to divide. This response suppresses opportunities for dialogue and greater understanding of the racial and cultural dynamics that exist on campus. It also allows anger and discouragement to build among students of color, because they do not have a forum in which to express themselves. This further widens the gap between the dominant majority and all minority groups.

EBC has a long history of viewing the Bible, rather than human reason, as the ultimate source of truth. This stance comes from its formation during the fundamentalist-modernist debates of the early twentieth century. However, since the Bible is interpreted from a highly individualistic perspective, the biblical passages promoting racial reconciliation and justice are largely ignored here. As a result, many suspect that promoting diversity is not addressed in the Bible and is instead part of a secular humanist perspective. Interestingly, however, when a biblical theology of racial justice is promoted, as in Mark Mori's programs, the result seems to be a group of people highly committed to racial justice and understanding how diverse perspectives can enrich an understanding of the Christian life.

Thus, this case does not necessarily suggest that viewing a religious text as the ultimate source of truth necessarily makes ethnic divisions more difficult to overcome. It depends on how that text is interpreted, and whether the insights of multiple perspectives on that text are valued. This case seems to illustrate how a specific religious tradition can create obstacles to racial integration even as it has within it the resources to overcome them.

Another key finding in our study of this campus was the high levels of relational isolation students of color experience. Since being embraced by fellow Christians is an important reason many students enroll in this college, students likely arrive here with higher expectations of finding belonging than students at secular colleges might have. The intensity of their isolation may also be heightened because of the importance of social contacts among late adolescents (Tatum 1997). As a result of this isolation of numerical minorities, students of color (with the exception of Asians) have higher turnover rates than white students. This is consistent with the other cases we have examined where numerical minorities have higher turnover rates than majority group members.

We also see similarities to other cases in the importance for numerical minorities of creating separate groups within the organization in which they might find support and belonging. Indeed, the multicultural program at this college served as the social lifeline for many students of color. This program has so far been the only initiative to provide a space for numerical minority groups to connect and talk about their experiences at the college.

Finally, we clearly see the impact of local and regional demographic transformations on this organization. Much like the cases of Wilcrest, Crosstown, and Brookside in their earlier years, the leaders of this predominantly white organization are beginning to be concerned that if they are not able to attract more non-whites, they may be in danger of losing enrollment in the future. Because it is a college, EBC will likely be able to continue to attract white students from other regions. Yet the demographic transformation of the surrounding area has prompted the school to begin looking for ways to better serve students of color, to avoid enrollment decline. It will be interesting to see whether these concerns result in efforts to move numerical minorities from the edge to the core of the organization.

8

What We Learned

We have covered a great deal of ground in our case studies, and we have visited a variety of places and religious organizations. For each case, we conducted around thirty in-depth face-to-face interviews with affiliates of religious organizations, including current members, former members, and leadership. We also observed religious meetings and "hung out" with members and leaders in less formal contexts. In doing so, we shared in the challenges, joys, and satisfaction that come with being a part of an interracial religious organization.

We have studied these organizations not just to get an inside look at them and gain a visceral understanding of the issues that confront them as they attempt to integrate, but also to make generalizations about the processes that occur in these social spaces. So in this chapter, we ask: what did we learn? We have focused primarily on the challenges these organizations face, paying specific attention to those forces that work to stabilize or destabilize them. We consider forces that facilitate the development or sustenance of racial integration in religious organizations to be stabilizing forces. Those forces that work against racial integration we call destabilizing forces. We categorize the forces affecting these organizations into three broad areas: internal organizational dynamics, external socioeconomic structures, and internal religious forces.

Internal Organizational Dynamics

In all of the organizations we have examined, we found that the ability of members to find belonging through friendship networks was a central problem. Because these are religious organizations, finding belonging is a much higher priority for members than would be the case in the workplace, for example. We found that the racial diversity of these organizations often complicated the ability of members to find belonging within them. As seen in five of the six cases, majority group members had a higher proportion of close friends from their own racial group than did minority group members. Also in five of six cases, majority group members had a higher proportion of their close friends within the organization than outside of it. For example, in the case of Messiah, where the numerical majority is Filipino, Filipinos were much more likely to name other Filipinos in the congregation as their closest friends. And compared to the non-Filipinos in the congregation, they had significantly less racial diversity among their close friends. What is more, their best friends were more likely to be within rather than outside the congregation. African Americans at Crosstown, the numerical majority group in that organization, were also more likely than white attenders to say that their closest friends were of their own race, and were more likely than whites to have their best friends within the church. We also found in each of our cases—at least in the early stages of the organizations' interracial transitions—that the turnover of numerical minorities was greater than for numerical majorities. These findings lead us to three general conclusions and a corollary:

> Other factors being equal, numerical majority group members have, within the religious organization, a higher percentage of close friends who are their same race, relative to the friendship racial backgrounds of minority group members.

> Other factors being equal, numerical majority group members have a higher percentage of close friends within the organization, relative to minority group members.

> Generally, within the religious organizations, turnover rates are higher for numerical minority groups than for majority groups.

> Insofar as the first three conclusions are true, interracial religious organizations are inherently unstable.

We expect that these conclusions generalize beyond our case studies, so we offer them as hypotheses to be tested further. The first conclusion is built into the very nature of relative group sizes: the larger the relative size of a group, the lower the rate of outgroup relations. For example, if we have an organization with eight blue and two orange people, and they have roughly the same number of friends, the blue people are less likely to have orange friends than the orange people are to have blue friends. Obviously, the greater the disparity in the relative size of groups, the more fully actualized is the statement that majority group members, relative to minority group members, will have same-race friends.

Our second and third conclusions make sense when put into theoretical context. Two processes are of particular importance: the *niche edge effect* and the *niche overlap effect*. We can define *niche* as the group(s) that an organization appeals to, attracts, or attempts to attract.

The *niche edge effect* means that members who are atypical of the organization—described as those who are at the edge of the organization rather than the core—leave at a higher rate than other members. We define core members as those belonging to the largest group(s), the group(s) having the most influence and power and sharing a visceral connection with the identity and mission of the organization. Because friendship ties and similarity with others influence membership duration in voluntary organizations (McPherson, Popielarz, and Drobnic 1992), members at the edge of the organization's niche will have a higher turnover rate than members at the core of the niche. This is a result of the fact that edge people, as compared to core people, have a higher proportion of ties outside the organization and a lower proportion of ties within it (Popielarz and McPherson 1995: 703). So in our mythical organization of eight blue and two orange people, the orange people typically will be at the edge of the organization. Because, as we have found in our case studies, the orange people will be more likely than the blue people to say that their best friends are located outside the religious organization, they will experience a continual pull to leave the organization for another where their orange friends are located.

Another factor that makes atypical members more likely to leave is the *niche overlap effect*. When the niches of organizations and groups partially overlap, they recruit some same-kind members. For the members being recruited simultaneously by multiple organizations—again, those on the edge and thus most dissimilar—the result is less stability of membership in any one group, because of finite access to time and other resources. Thus, even if atypical members have ties within an organization, they can have high turnover rates because the pressure for them to join other organizations, generated by those organizations' attempts to woo them away from their current affiliations, is more intense than it is for core group members. Not only are orange members in our mythical organization likely to have more ties outside of our organization than within it; they are also more likely to closely fit the niches of other organizations—especially those catering to oranges—than the niches of our multicolored organization. An important exception is if they are "cross-color-tied"—for example, if an orange is married to a blue. In such instances, the orange person is less likely to be at the niche edge of the multicolored organization. This means that an important niche—and one interracial organizations are uniquely positioned to reach—are interracial families and interracial people (whether by blood or experience). We discuss this further below. Interracial congregations are heavily set in niche overlap space, as they draw members from a variety of groups that also have homogeneous organizations recruiting them. So competition is intensified. Other things being equal, then, niche edge and niche overlap effects conspire to produce higher turnover for congregational minorities, constantly putting interracial organizations at risk and making them unstable.

How then is it possible to have stable interracial congregations? Our cases hint at an answer. Consider for example the case of Wilcrest. Turnover was higher for numerical minorities (at times, dramatically so), but the rate of numerical minority visitors, for the variety of reasons we explored in chapter 3, was usually higher than the rate of members leaving. Efforts also were instituted to draw edge people in toward the core, not in terms of assimilation but in terms of influence, social ties, and structural changes (e.g., changes in musical styles and programs offered, greater representation in leadership). Over time, then, numerical minorities grew both in absolute and relative numbers. As they did, such members moved away from the edge and toward the core, reducing the destabilizing impact of the niche edge and niche overlap effects.

At Messiah we saw a similar dynamic. Numerical minority members left the organization at higher rates than did members of the majority. Yet the non-Filipinos who left were quickly replaced by new visitors and new members. Despite a high turnover rate among non-Filipinos, the percentage of non-Filipinos at the church has remained fairly stable. At Emmanuel Bible College, despite a lower retention rate among black and Hispanic students, the percentage of minority students has remained fairly stable due to its location in a region that has become majority non-white.

If an organization achieves a sufficient number of minorities (where "sufficient" is best understood as an interaction between the relative and absolute size of groups) it can stabilize. It can reach a point where multiple groups become core members and recruit new members through their networks, and where visitors from various groups feel welcomed. An example is the case of Crosstown, the oldest interracial organization we studied. Once a white congregation, Crosstown clearly has more than one core group. African Americans now constitute the majority, but whites remain a significant percentage of the congregation; the senior minister is African American, the youth minister is white; the leadership is racially diverse; and elements of multiple worship styles are used in the services.

We found a potential destabilizing force in the process of achieving a sufficient number of edge members, which may be called the "great reversal." Former edge groups may become so large that they render initial core members edge members, pushing the organization to begin again the process of differential turnover. As we will see in the next section, this is especially problematic when white members move from core to edge.

We qualify these conclusions with clauses, like "other things being equal," or "generally," because other factors matter in these processes. The number of friends people have inside the religious organization as opposed to outside the organization, and thus turnover rates and the stability of interracial organizations, can also be influenced by how long people have been in the organization. This is especially germane if duration of membership differs by group, as it often does.

More importantly, we found that the gap between groups in the number of friends inside versus outside the organization varied. We found large gaps in organizations such as Wilcrest, Messiah, and Christ in Action. We found a smaller gap at Crosstown. This discrepancy points to an exception to our second conclusion, and perhaps to the third and fourth as well. The United States is a highly mobile society.

Anyone who has ever moved to a new, unfamiliar place knows the need to find rootedness, connection, and friendships. For those in such situations congregations become not just places to worship but vital locations for establishing friendships, connecting with social networks, and gaining a sense of belonging. To put it more bluntly, mobile people are more needy than people who have stayed in the same general area most of their lives and already have well-established social ties. All organizations but one in our study included in their membership a significant proportion of people who were movers or migrants. The exception was Crosstown, most of whose members either grew up in the local area or had spent a significant portion of their lives there. For them the congregation was less vital for friendships than it was for members of the other organizations studied.

This realization leads us to a hypothesis beyond our data, but one we think must be studied in future work:

Mobility heightens the need for the congregation to provide for relational and social needs. Therefore, in light of the increased difficulty in obtaining these in interracial congregations, mobility reduces the opportunity for sustainable integration of people within organizations that provide belonging and meaning.

Mobility can bring diverse peoples into proximate space, but at the same time it intensifies conditions that require interracial organizations to fulfill belonging and meaning functions. Religious organizations, then, have to find ways to provide for people's needs. This mandate includes, most certainly, efforts directed toward developing cross-racial networks among members.

However, in some of our cases (e.g., Crosstown), we learned that friendly cross-racial ties within a religious organization are not a sufficient guard against racial transitioning. Contact theory has much to say about the positive effects that can be expected from contact between people of different racial groups, provided that four conditions are satisfied: support from superiors (such as religious leaders), a common goal, cooperative rather than competitive orientation, and nonsuperficial relations. Certainly, religious organizations can meet these four conditions much if not most of the time; therefore, contact theory would predict very positive outcomes for such organizations, including increased appreciation of the out groups, more positive attitudes, and even a desire to be with one another.

But such ties, we found, tend not to be sufficient to overcome the niche edge and niche overlap effects. People can feel personally warm toward one another, but social factors larger than individual relationships appear to overcome these cross-racial ties. For transitioning not to occur, more stabilizers are needed, such as increased growth and representation of the edge groups.

In part because of the isolation that can be experienced by an edge group or person, we learned over and over in our case studies that while benefits of the diverse environment were rather evenly distributed across people and groups within the organizations, the costs were disproportionately borne by edge people. This suggests the following hypothesis:

> Numerical minority group members bear the highest relational costs of being involved in interracial organizations. The costs are reduced as representation increases.

To be part of interracial organizations is risky. To the degree that a congregation is a source of support, consolation, celebration, and strength, if persons do not feel integrated into the congregation, if their worth or troubles are devalued, if people like them are scarce—in other words, if they occupy the niche edge—they lose compared to what they could receive in racially homogeneous congregations.

As we have seen, the larger the group, the lower the rate of outgroup relations. Conversely, smaller groups' probability of outgroup relations increases, so that minority group members must derive more meaning and belonging from their relations with members of other groups. This puts persons of smaller groups at greater risk for failure to meet their needs for meaning and belonging (and, we should add, greater potential of crossing group boundaries, if successful). These effects are amplified in smaller congregations, or in congregations in which the number of people in one's own cultural group is small in absolute terms. In all, although integration can promote positive social relations and social mobility within the organization as a whole, for the subgroups it appears that majority members largely experience benefits (their needs are easily met by same-race members, so the addition of "diversity" is experienced largely as an additional positive to the congregation), whereas minority members experience both costs and benefits (they venture across racial boundaries not just for enjoyment and novelty, but to gain meaning and belonging, which entails more effort and more risk).

Different ways to cope with this greater effort and risk are available to edge people. Perhaps the most common is to simply leave. However, in the case of the campus group, the students of color at Emmanuel Bible College, the Spanish speakers at Wilcrest, and black and Hispanic members at Brookside, we found another solution: form a subgroup within the larger organization. The African Americans in the campus group formed a subgroup with its own name, meeting times, styles, and networks. It focused on catering to African Americans. Though under the umbrella of the national organization to which the campus group belongs, in the African American group is, in most senses, a separate local organization. Less dramatically, the Spanish speakers at Wilcrest minimized costs by forming a Latino Sunday school class, offering translation of services, and organizing some separate social or fund-raising events. While very much a part of Wilcrest, they have also created some "safe" social space to meet their needs. The 11 o'clock service at Brookside functioned in this way as well.

Concentrating all of the non-white members into one service minimized the costs that black and Latino members faced in this predominantly white organization. At Emmanuel Bible College, the multi-ethnic programs group ameliorated to some extent the pain and loneliness felt by students of color.

We did not find examples of whites who were in the minority forming groups to minimize costs. In the next section we explore their tendency to use other solutions—such as leaving. But this points us to another conclusion from our research.

> The importance of minimizing the costs of being in interracial organizations is greatest for those who are racial minorities in the larger society, because they pay the costs of both numerical and minority statuses daily in the larger society.

In addition to leaving (from the organizational viewpoint, this is not a viable solution), forming separate sub-organizations, and carving out separate group time, we found other important means of minimizing costs. As we hypothesized, the costs are reduced as representation increases. Representation can be in any or all of the following areas: raw numbers, worship styles, leadership, or organizational practices. For instance, incorporating music from the out group's culture, increasing diversity in the staff, accommodating different attitudes and understandings of time, and instituting children's programs are all examples of increasing representation, depending on which groups are marginalized. Increasing representation and providing some time for separate space for groups are the means organizations are most able to control.

Our cases repeatedly pointed us to another finding. Individual racial views and prejudices matter, but they seem to play a small role in the experiences of interracial religious groups. We listened carefully to what edge people said about why they came to these organizations, why they stayed or left, and how they perceived their experiences. We found that whether they felt welcomed or excluded had less to do with individual expressions than with structural expressions of inclusion. This leads us to the following hypotheses:

> The rejection felt by numerical minorities is more strongly related to the size of the majority group than to the individual racial views of majority members.

The acceptance felt by numerical minorities is related to the structural inclusion they witness, such as the vision statement of the organization, the worship styles, leadership representation, and other structural arrangements.

Our cases are replete with examples in support of these hypotheses. With the exception of students of color at Emmanuel Bible College, rarely did we hear that someone left an organization or felt excluded because an individual or individuals acted in a discriminatory or disrespectful way toward them. Virtually everyone we talked to recognized that such individuals exist, but they were able to dismiss or deal with such instances as simple anomalies. What matters much more than what people say in one-on-one interactions is what the organization does or does not do structurally to include people. If people are treated interpersonally nicely and warmly, but leadership comprises only one group, and worship and other organizational practices reflect the styles and preferences of that same group, edge members feel the costs of membership more acutely.

Not all numerical groups experience costs to the same degree, and this has implications for what types of interracial congregations are more likely to be sustainable. Our findings also suggest that the greater the number of racial and ethnic groups in the organization, the less people expect to see representation of their own specific group. It may also be that the greater the number of groups, the less acutely they feel or the more willing they are to bear the costs, since it is clear that other groups too have to sacrifice. If misery loves company, perhaps the same is true for bearing costs. Moreover, with more than two groups, the dominance of any single group may seem reduced. We can only offer this as a tentative statement, as our cases are only suggestive on this matter.

Disagreements over how the organizations were structured were often sources of conflict. This is true, of course, of all organizations, but the fact that these organizations were interracial seemed to produce additional conflicts that would not exist in a homogeneous organization. As Naylor (1999) states:

As culture represents truth, when people of different cultures come together, the consequence must always be some conflict, for it is more than people coming into contact. It really means that truths come into contact and that means conflict. Each group tends to believe that its beliefs and practices are the right or more correct ones. They judge others by it and being convinced of its correctness, each group makes every effort to impose their truth on everybody else. As everybody does the same thing, cultural contact will always mean conflict.

This statement would apply to all interracial organizations, but as we discuss further below, religious organizations seem particularly susceptible to conflict because of the heightened tendency to hold absolute positions on the rightness or wrongness of a particular action, due to the religious nature of the organization. Conflict seems to be intensified when all of the members are committed to the absolute truth of their beliefs, but the various cultural groups within the organization differ on how those beliefs are lived out.

Cultural conflicts in the groups we studied tended to play themselves out in disagreements over how the organization was structured. In the case of Messiah fellowship, for example, white members of the congregation felt that the church was too lax and not organized enough. They felt, for example, that the Sunday school program for children did not have consistent teachers, a standardized curriculum, or enough organized activities for the children. They also felt that there were not enough organized programs for evangelism, outreach to the community, or caring for church members. Filipino members, however, were quite happy with the way the organization was structured and felt that whites were unnecessarily focused on planning, meetings, and bureaucracy. Both groups felt strongly about the rightness of their way of doing things. At Emmanuel Bible College, students of color felt that the organization was structured around a highly individualistic faith, rather than on the building of community and the pursuit of justice and mutual understanding. Moreover, they felt that the knowledge being promoted did not address the concerns most central to their lives and their faith. The white majority, however, felt strongly that their understanding of the faith was "biblical" and that deviations from that understanding were rooted in error.

All of the organizations we studied experienced particular conflicts between ethnic groups regarding some aspects of how the organization operated. However, there were differences in the extent to which different cultural styles were integrated into the workings of the organizations. At one end of the continuum, Brookside's 11 o'clock service has a staff whose members represent all three of the major ethnic groups at the church (Hispanic, black, white). These staff members are able to preach, lead music, and minister to people using cultural styles from their respective ethnic groups. At the other end of the continuum, Emmanuel Bible College had a staff that was almost exclusively white, and spiritual and curricular activities therefore were almost exclusively embedded in the subculture of white evangelicalism.

The minority experience in organizations led by one dominant ethnic group seemed to be much more painful and frustrating than in those that had not only integrated their leadership staff, but also integrated different cultural styles into the way the organization operated. This leads to the following hypothesis:

Organizations that have a diverse leadership staff are more able to satisfy multiple constituent groups within the organization, thus lessening the overall level of conflict.

When we assess the dynamics operating within organizations that are attempting to integrate, we find both destabilizing and stabilizing forces. The destabilizing forces include the following:

1. Niche edge effect (edge members leave faster than core members)
2. Niche overlap effect (more outside competition for edge members)
3. Lack of group representation
4. Costs borne disproportionately by numerical minorities

The stabilizing forces include the following:

1. "Adequate" sizes of respective groups
2. More than two groups
3. Diverse representation in leadership, worship, and other structures

External Socioeconomic Structures

Interracial religious organizations do not stand alone. They are affected by the society in which we live. Social factors and the expectations of secular society influence how these religious organizations work, who attends them, and who will remain. From our case studies, we have isolated several factors that affect the racial stability of these organizations, all of which are rooted in the dominant social, economic, and cultural status of whites in the larger society. We have found that these factors make it more difficult for interracial religious organizations to retain white membership. Therefore, a primary issue interracial religious organizations must address if they are going to remain interracial is how they will continue to attract and retain white members in the face of inhibitory social structural forces.

The Local Community

The social and economic outcomes for religious organizations depend upon the financial and human resources available in local communities (Ammerman 1997). The demographic conditions of the local environment impact the membership of locally oriented religious organizations (Hadaway 1981). This is particularly true for interracial religious organizations. As Wedam et al. (1999) and Emerson and Kim (2003) demonstrate, changes in the racial composition of neighborhoods are often the impetus for racial change within neighborhood churches.

In four of the six case studies—Crosstown Baptist Church, Wilcrest Community Church, Brookside Community Church, and Christ in Action—we see this dynamic in action. For the three churches, the idea of becoming interracial and adopting an interracial identity was not entertained until after the local neighborhoods surrounding them began to experience white flight. The local neighborhood of Wilcrest experienced rapid white flight between 1980 and 2000, transitioning from more than 90 percent white to 90 percent Latino, African American. and Asian. The neighborhood in which Brookside is located similarly transitioned from predominantly white in 1970 to 85 percent Latino and African American in 2000. Although the Crosstown neighborhood has remained the most integrated of the three, including both Mapleton and Anderson, the racial composition of the community around Crosstown has transitioned from nearly all white in 1960 to 70 percent African American, 25 percent Latino, and 5 percent Asian in 2000.[1] During the time that white flight was occurring in these neighborhoods, all these churches experienced a decline in membership. All were confronted with the real possibility of having to close their doors. As Finke and Stark (1992) predicted, these churches moved toward racially integrating their congregations only when faced with a crisis.

Wilcrest and Brookside have successfully negotiated the ecological changes in their neighborhoods. They have continued to be racially integrated congregations despite near complete racial successions in their local communities. The congregations have sustained racial integration because they have transitioned from locally oriented churches to regional churches. While some congregational members come from the local neighborhood, many others (most of whom are white) come from other communities in the metropolitan area, as far as forty miles away.

However, religious organizations that cannot or have not established a regional orientation find it difficult to escape the impact of neighborhood racial change on the racial composition of their organization. This leads us to another hypothesis:

Interracial religious organizations that have a local geographic orientation are restricted in their capacity to develop and maintain a racially diverse membership.

To the extent that the local community is racially heterogeneous, the religious organization can develop and sustain a racially diverse membership. The racial composition of locally oriented congregations is dependent upon that of the surrounding community. For example, if the surrounding community becomes predominantly black, the religious organization, despite its desire to remain interracial, is likely to follow a similar pattern. On the other hand, regional churches, since they are not oriented toward their surrounding communities, at least have a broader geographic area from which to draw potential attenders. The pool of people from various racial backgrounds will likely be larger than that of community churches.

Crosstown is an example of a religious organization that has remained a locally oriented church. Seventy percent of its regular attenders live in Mapleton or Anderson. The church has intentionally changed its geographic orientation toward the surrounding neighborhoods. It is decidedly a neighborhood church, rather than a regional church. Hence, the church's racial composition is linked to that of the local community. Consequently, the church's racial composition is quite close to that of the surrounding community. The racial composition of Mapleton and Anderson combined is 69 percent African American, 25 percent white, and 6 percent Asian, Latino, and Native American. Crosstown is about 65 percent African American and 30 percent white. Furthermore, the proportion of

African American members has steadily increased in the church over the past two decades as the proportion of African Americans in the neighborhood has increased. This demonstrates that although neighborhood change can be the catalyst for racial inclusion in American churches, it can also be a deterrent. A possible saving grace for Crosstown is that Mapleton has instituted policies to facilitate interracial neighborhood stabilization. As long as Mapleton enacts these policies, Crosstown will have a racially diverse local population from which to draw. However, this is a rare occurrence in American neighborhoods. Most interracial religious organizations will at some point in their history likely need to become regionally oriented.

In the case of Brookside, a highly loyal white membership commutes from surrounding suburbs and thus maintains a dominant white presence there despite the almost complete absence of whites in the local neighborhood. As Brookside is relatively early in its racial integration process, it is still too early to tell whether these whites will continue attending as the process unfolds. The leadership seems well aware of the possibility of a "great reversal" and has therefore been careful not to alienate the white membership. This is one reason for concentrating efforts to integrate the church in just one of the three church services.

Christ in Action and Reach are also dependent upon the racial composition of their local community. However, for these types of organizations, the university campus serves as the local community. This is particularly true for these student organizations because they draw largely from students who are also campus residents. To the extent that the university can successfully attract and retain a racially diverse student body, religious student organizations can similarly be interracial. We do not have longitudinal data on the racial composition of South Urban University campus specifically, or on the student organizations. However, Christ in Action decided to develop race- or ethnic-specific sub-organizations in response to the changes in the racial composition of university campuses. Like the three churches discussed above, this religious organization developed measures to become racially and ethnically inclusive after changes occurred in the local community. Unlike congregations, however, religious student organizations are less likely to adopt a regional orientation, as they are organized around having a student identity.

The case of Emmanuel Bible College is slightly different. As a college, it draws from a wider geographic region than the other organizations we studied. Consequently, it is less susceptible to the effects of racial transitioning in the surrounding neighborhood. In fact, the percentage of white students has actually increased slightly in the last eight years, even though the neighborhood and region in which it is located has transitioned to majority non-white over that same period. However, the location of the college has forced it to grapple with its decreasing enrollment percentage and lower retention rate among students of color precisely because its demographic trends are going against the surrounding region. This trend has caused campus administrators to worry whether the organization will be able to survive in a multi-ethnic market and has led to some efforts to address diversity issues on campus. Thus, even in this case, the demographics of the surrounding neighborhood and region have powerfully affected the organization.

The Expanding Population of Interracial Families

One of the most consistent findings in our case studies is that individuals from biracial and interracial families felt particularly comfortable in the interracial organizations we studied. Many of those who were in interracial marriages reported that both partners felt comfortable in these interracial organizations. In numerous cases interracial couples had been to a number of homogeneous groups and one of the spouses inevitably felt uncomfortable and out of place. These couples reported that in diverse settings they felt like they "didn't stand out" and "felt like home."

For biracial and interracial families with children, this feeling of "home" was particularly salient. They expressed relief that they had found a place where their children did not stand out and could more readily fit in with other children.

This highlights an interesting phenomenon. For those from racially and ethnically homogeneous backgrounds, the costs involved in participating in an interracial organization often included not feeling at home and having to adjust to different cultural styles of expressing and living out their faith. Thus, they often valued the diversity of the church, but the value they placed on diversity was always counterbalanced by the costs of not feeling at home. Biracial and interracial families, however, not only placed a high value on diversity, but also experienced a sense of feeling more at home in an interracial organization than in a homogeneous one.

This was the case for those who grew up in diverse environments as well. A small number of our respondents reported that they had grown up in interracial neighborhoods and attended interracial schools. These respondents reported feeling uncomfortable in homogeneous religious groups because such groups were so different from what they had grown up with.

The literature on the population ecology of organizations suggests that the survival of an organization is determined by its "fitness" to its external environment (Hannan and Freeman 1977; Carroll 1984; Singh and Lumsden 1990). As the number of interracial families in America continues to increase, and as the diversity of certain metropolitan areas increases, interracial religious organizations will likely have a greater degree of fitness in those environments.

For an increasing number of Americans, home is a racially and ethnically diverse place. The number of interracial marriages increased tenfold from 1960 to 1998—from 149,000 in 1960 to 1.4 million in 1998. While this still represents less than 3 percent of all marriages in the United States, the numbers continue to grow; and in some states, most notably California, interracial marriages account for close to 10 percent of all marriages (all figures from the U.S. Census Bureau). If members of this growing population become participants in interracial religious organizations they will likely be more committed to staying than those who come from homogeneous families and backgrounds. This leads to the following hypotheses:

> Other factors being equal, the higher the proportion of an organization's members from biracial/interracial families and/or backgrounds, the lower the rate of membership turnover and therefore the more stable the organization.

> Other factors being equal, the higher the proportion of interracial neighborhoods and interracial marriages in a region, the higher the rate of both founding and survival of interracial religious organizations will be in that region.

The demographic trends of growing numbers of interracial marriages and interracial neighborhoods and schools thus create a growing niche for interracial religious organizations to serve. This will most likely result in the founding and survival of more and more interracial religious organizations in the future.

Effects of Institutionalized White Dominance .

We found repeatedly that it is more difficult for interracial religious organizations to retain their white membership as compared to other groups. In other words, whites are more likely to leave interracial churches than are nonwhites. We saw that whites leave religious organizations for several reasons. One is that they move out of state, usually for better job opportunities or to live closer to extended family. Whites appear to be more mobile than other groups, a finding consistent with the mobility literature (Frey 1985; Rossi 1980; Tucker and Urton 1987). Therefore, we also propose that

> Holding group sizes constant, whites are more likely to leave interracial religious organizations than are members of other groups. At least a portion of this effect is due to higher rates of non-local mobility among whites.

Mobility of members is an issue that any religious organization has to face, regardless of its racial composition, especially if it consists largely of people who are still in critical stages of their careers. However, as whites have greater economic mobility and opportunities than racial minorities, there tends to be a disproportionate out-migration of whites compared to racial minorities. For churches that place their interracial status at the center of their identity, this process of migration is of great importance. This is not to say that people of color, if given the same economic opportunities, would not leave. Some respondents of color reported that they would leave the church if a better job opportunity presented itself. It is rather the reality that such opportunities are less common among racial minorities than among whites.

Generally, within religious organizations, turnover rates are higher for numerical minority groups than for majority groups. As we have already discussed, a possible antidote to this is to intentionally draw numerical minority members into the core of the church, so that they are no longer edge members. In most cases, interracial religious organizations began with a predominantly white membership. Therefore, at the beginning of the racial transitioning process whites are the numerical majority in the organization and constitute most if not all of the core group of the organization. Edge members tend to be from racial minority groups. Over time, as racial minorities increase numerically and gain entry into the core group, the organization has the potential of stabilizing. However, we have found that as whites approach becoming the numerical minority, their turnover rates increase. The process that dictates higher turnover rates for numerical minority groups, overall, is intensified. We have found that this outcome is due to the following:

> Whites are more likely than racial minorities to leave interracial religious organizations if their particular preferences and interests are not being met.

This conclusion manifests itself most poignantly in three areas of congregational life. One is the worship service style and organization. When whites' perception of what constitutes the ideal or appropriate kind of worship service is not actualized, they tend to leave rather than to collaborate on worship styles or preferences. At Wilcrest, whites began to leave the church once Latino and African American music styles began to be incorporated into the worship service. One of these white members, a longtime deacon of the church, expressed particular disdain for styles of music other than those he preferred, going so far as to say that these alternative styles were "just not right." This member ultimately left the church. At Messiah, a number of white members who were initially excited about the diversity of the congregation left because they felt the church was not organized enough.

Secondly, strong network ties and integral participation of racial minorities in interracial religious organizations is of particular concern for whites; such ties are often interpreted as exclusionary. In both Messiah and Christ in Action, the relationally dense and relatively influential Asian groups in the organizations were considered cliquish and in some cases counter to diversity. Similarly, white Christ in Action students expressed concerns about the purpose of race-specific groups such as Reach. Whites either left or contemplated leaving the organizations because they felt these groups were exclusionary.

Another phenomenon that emerged from our study and discussion of the cases is that the children's and youth programs of interracial churches tend to be disproportionately nonwhite relative to the population of the church.[2] For example, among the seventy adolescents and teenagers in Wilcrest's youth group, only about five are white. Crosstown's youth program of about twenty middle- and high-school-aged youth is all black, except for two children. Although Messiah has no youth program, their children's program is less than 10 percent white.

The disproportionate representation of non-white children in the youth and children's programs is in part because there are few white families in these organizations who have children in the home, especially children of dating age. Whites who attend interracial churches tend to be single, recently married couples or couples with adult children. While at first this may appear to be a rather benign explanation for the vacuum of white families with school-aged children, the reality is that whites are likely to leave interracial religious organizations once they have school-aged children, particularly children who have reached dating age.[3] Old ideas and stereotypes appear to die hard.

Therefore, dissatisfaction with the organization and characteristics of the youth and children's programs was a third area of concern among whites; for some, it was their primary reason for leaving. White parents of adolescent and teenage children expressed the most critical judgments about these programs. In our interviews, white parents rarely cited race as a specific reason for their concerns about the children's or youth groups. Rather, they expressed concerns about their children's ability to reach their full potential in youth groups that are, at least from their perspective, composed predominantly of non-Christian, "hard-core," or loud children. Given that these groups are mostly made up of children of color, we can reasonably infer that they are not referring to whites in these descriptions. Parents explained that their children were unable to relate to their non-white peers or to develop friendships with other children in the children's or youth group. In addition to their social lives, parents also claim that their children's spiritual growth was suffering in the predominantly non-white children's or youth groups. Moreover, the non-white children in these groups did not have the kinds of values they wanted to instill in their children, such as valuing education. In some cases, white parents of preschool-aged children expressed concerns about the racial composition of the children's or youth groups even as they were already considering the possibility of leaving the church if these groups didn't change. One parent in particular told us she was already "nervous" about the kinds of experiences and possible lack of opportunities her children would experience in the youth group if its composition remained as it was. When the children of these families approach adolescence, and in some cases when they are just approaching school age, the concerned parents leave interracial churches for predominantly white churches with predominantly white youth and children's groups, even though they believe that attending an interracial church is valuable for them personally. Therefore, we have concluded that:

> White adults, despite their desire to attend an interracial church and their belief that this membership holds intrinsic benefits for them, are unwilling to sacrifice the potential experiences, privileges and opportunities of their children to do so.

For white families who have to consider the impact on their children of attending an interracial church, multiracial interaction ceases to be a priority in selecting a church.

The irony of this is that the non-white children in these groups are largely Christian (or children of other church families) and middle-class. Moreover, the children's and youth programs of these churches would not be predominantly non-white if these families remained. White parents sometimes made racist assumptions about the ability and values of the children in the children's and youth groups, drawing upon preconceived notions of minority cultural characteristics and racial stereotypes. They relied upon distant rather than proximate knowledge of the children in the groups to inform their understanding and provide a basis for leaving the church.

The concerns of these white parents echo those expressed in Johnson and Shapiro's (2003) work on white families' reasons for choosing neighborhoods and schools.[4] They found race to be fundamental to white families' choices about schools and where to live. Although the white families in that study were far more explicit in their racial prejudices than were the parents in our case studies, whites tend to perceive non-whites as inferior, ascribing such traits to them as poor, drug addicted, or people who devalue education. Therefore, interracial or predominantly non-white neighborhoods are perceived to be detrimental to them and their children's life chances. Our study reveals that white families' choices of where to worship are guided by similar prejudices.

Whites concerns about the culture and organization of their churches (or previous churches in many cases), while in part motivated by personal preferences, beliefs, and desires, are also motivated by how they believe other whites will perceive them. This leads us to another conclusion:

Maintaining legitimacy within the dominant group is of greater priority for whites than are the desires and needs of fellow non-white organization members.

Recall the case of the deacon at Wilcrest. His disdain for the introduction of new music styles into the worship service was not just about personal preference. He explained that he would be "embarrassed" to bring friends to the church with the new kind of music that had been introduced. The white students in Christ in Action were concerned that the proportion of Asians in the organization would discourage other whites from joining the group. Again, they were more concerned about the preferences of other whites than about those of their Asian "brothers" and "sisters." They maintained these concerns, despite Asians' lack of presence in nearly every other context on campus. What is profound about this perspective is its implication that whites should be in control in all situations.

At Messiah fellowship, white people seemed to have a greater desire to have their interests reflected in the organization than did the other numerical minority groups in the church. They were also more likely to volunteer for leadership positions with the hope of changing the organization to better fit their expectations. When those hopes were not realized, many left. Compared to other numerical minority groups, whites seemed to have a greater expectation that the organization would be run according to their standards. In addition, interestingly, the non-white leadership of the organization seemed to take more notice of the complaints of whites than of those of other minority groups within the congregation.

People of color also mentioned frustrations or concerns about their experiences as members of interracial churches. While not at the same rate as whites, people of color also left churches because of their particular concerns. However, we found that racial minorities were far more aware of the necessity for compromise in an interracial setting and were far more willing to compromise, to yield their own desires or preferences in situations of conflict. Fernando's willingness to return to Wilcrest after being blatantly excluded from a church activity is just one example. The absence of their specific cultural preferences, beliefs, or values is usually not a sufficient reason for minority members to leave interracial churches. Their greater willingness to compromise or yield to the desires of whites is likely the result of regularly having to accommodate whites in almost all other contexts. For most white Americans, however, being in a context where they are expected to accommodate the preferences and desires of racial minorities is rare indeed. Having to do so is a rather foreign experience.

Whites are accustomed to being in control in social contexts. Their norms and values are in most cases accepted without challenge. These characteristics afford whites far greater opportunity, relative to racial minorities, to live in, establish, and reproduce social spaces that accommodate their preferences, culture, and superior status (Bonilla-Silva 2001; Doane 2003; Feagin, Vera, and Batur 2001; Frankenburg 1993; Omi and Winant 1997). Therefore, when whites do not have disproportionate control in the organization (in the form of leadership positions, for example); when their worship preferences and customs are not accommodated; or when their ability to reproduce their cultural practices and values in their children is hindered, they are more likely than non-whites to express concerns. If the organization does not address concerns, and in fact capitulate to white people's wishes, it is easy for the white people in question to find other organizations that will, and so they leave interracial churches in pursuit of this. Reflecting upon examples from the cases in this study, we see the difficulty whites have in adjusting to challenges to white control.

However, whites are not necessarily aware of their privileged status as the dominant racial group, nor are they aware how their own actions perpetuate it. According to scholar George Lipsitz, "the artificial construction of whiteness almost always comes to possess white people themselves unless they develop antiracist identities" (1998: vii). Unless whites are conscious of the status and privileges afforded them through whiteness, and unless they act to dismantle the structure that sustains that privilege, they will by default reproduce the racialized social order. Consequently, white members' decisions to leave interracial churches, whether seeking socioeconomic mobility, reacting to dissatisfaction with the worship service, expressing discomfort with strong non-white presence, or seeking to protect their children from the supposed negative influences of non-white children, are a response to the unconscious expectations and understanding of what it means to be white—that is, to exist in a social environment where they are in control and their ways of life are dominant. In their belief that their norms, values, and beliefs are superior to those of racial minority groups and in their subsequent retreat to predominantly white congregations, whites reproduce whiteness.

Unfortunately, the disproportionate departure of whites from interracial churches acts not only to destabilize the racial balance in the church, but also to undermine the faith of racial minorities in the possibility of interracial social contexts, to belie minorities' trust that religiously rooted whites would be more accepting of and invested in racial integration than other whites.

In summary, the dominant status of whites in the external socioeconomic structures of American society produces the following destabilizing forces:

1. Higher mobility rates among whites
2. Higher expectations among whites rthat their preferences and interests will be met
3. White parents' unwillingness to have their children participate in majority non-white youth programs
4. White concern with maintaining legitimacy

These forces all lead to higher turnover rates for whites in interracial religious organizations where other racial groups are moving to the core, thus making retaining white membership a key concern for interracial religious organizations.

The one external force that we found to produce stability is that increasing numbers of interracial families creates a niche where interracial religious organizations have an advantage over homogeneous organizations.

Internal Religious Dynamics

We also found powerful spiritual and religious forces affecting these organizations. Some of these forces served to stabilize the organization and others had a destabilizing effect.

Religiously Charged Ethnocentrism

Because these organizations are religious in nature, their members tend to interpret most of life through a religiously informed grid. As we have seen, differences in culture are often given absolute and transcendent meanings. This is illustrated through the debate over the way Messiah fellowship's church service is timed. Time-oriented white members felt not only that the lax timing of the church service was inconvenient for them, but also that it was a sign of disrespect toward God. Likewise, African Americans and Filipinos who preferred a more flexible schedule felt that rigidly timing a service was squelching the Holy Spirit. Framing this cultural issue in absolute terms raises the stakes considerably—arguments over cultural differences quickly become arguments about God. We suspect that this dynamic produces more conflict and less opportunity for compromise on issues of differing cultural values than would exist in a nonreligious organization.

Furthermore, all religious expression is embedded in particular cultural forms, so individuals experience God through culturally specific media. In evangelical Protestantism, worship music is a key component of "connecting to God" in a church service. Thus, differences in musical preference and worship styles get framed in absolute terms. This raises the stakes in conflicts over music styles and forms of expression, as each group feels their particular style is more conducive to "connecting to God" or to "being transformed" by the experience.

Many white members of the organizations we studied felt that worship was not "reverent" enough. Non-whites often complained that white styles of worship music were "dead," "rigid," and "left you unchanged." Religious expressions, therefore, that are always embedded in particular cultural forms can lead to the deification of those cultural forms themselves as cultural attributes take on religious meanings.

The sociologist Emile Durkheim, in his classic *The Elementary Forms of Religious Life,* argued that human societies essentially worship themselves through religion. Through studying totemism among the Australian Arunta tribe, he concluded that their religion, and religion in general, is derived from the collective morality of its host society, rather than through an outside spiritual force. According to Durkheim (1912: 250), "religious force is nothing other than the collective and anonymous force of the clan." Whether or not one believes that religion is nothing more than a human society worshipping its own collective morality (we do not), it is clear that the dynamic Durkheim identified is at work in our cases.

For example, the Anglo-American moral value placed on such things as punctuality, order, organization, and rationality clearly, in our cases, becomes more than a matter of humans giving them value for practical reasons. These values become associated with the sacred, and as a result going against them becomes more than simply a disagreement over human preferences. It becomes a violation of the sacred, as is witnessed in the language used to describe those who show up late: they were viewed as irreverent, as disrespecting God. Whether God wants everyone at church exactly on time or wants a highly organized, efficient bureaucracy is clearly not addressed in the historic documents or doctrines of the Christian faith. Yet they become part of the Christian faith for those whose culture holds these values to be important.

This *religiously charged ethnocentrism* was evident in all of the organizations we studied. The ubiquity of this phenomenon in our cases leads us to the following hypothesis:

> Interracial religious organizations have higher levels of conflict than interracial nonreligious organizations because cultural differences tend to be given absolute and transcendent meanings, making compromise more difficult.

This may explain in part the higher levels of segregation among religious organizations in America as opposed to other types of organizations.

Theological Arguments for Color-Blindness and Multiculturalism

An important destabilizing force that was found to a greater or lesser degree in all of our cases was a theologically driven argument for "color-blindness" that promotes the idea that unity among believers comes from emphasizing commonalities rather than differences. A number of respondents we interviewed, particularly white respondents, expressed that in order for unity to flourish among the members of the organization, differences must be downplayed and commonalities emphasized. Statements such as "God doesn't see color" and "our identity is in Christ, not in our ethnicity" seemed to suggest that difference must be suppressed in order to achieve unity. Some members of these organizations bristled at the mention of cultural differences or racial issues. "Let's focus on what the Bible says, not on these unimportant issues that divide us" was a refrain among some. At the evangelical college this ideology seemed particularly strong, to the point that students of color complained of a strong backlash and accusations of divisiveness when racial issues were addressed.

This color-blind ideology was not necessarily an idea intentionally promoted by the leadership of any of the organizations we studied. As Emerson and Smith (2000) and Bonilla-Silva (2000) suggest, however, it is central to the way white Americans think about racial problems. This ideology is essentially individualistic because identifying oneself as a member of a group rather than as an individual is seen as the source of divisions and conflict among groups. Emerson and Smith (2000) also argue that the white evangelical subculture intensifies this individualism because of its emphasis on individual accountability before God. In this subculture, it is believed that the individual, not culture or social structures, determines the outcome of one's life. As a result, attempts to address cultural differences or institutional inequality are seen as shifting blame from the individual to society and producing unnecessary divisions between groups.

We found that this color-blind ideology among whites as well as in some other non-white groups led to a reluctance to engage in dialogue about racial issues in some of the organizations. Members of the organization that held to a theologically based color-blindness, particularly those in the majority, reacted negatively to public dialogues and presentations about racial issues. In the case of the evangelical college, it led to the feeling among students of color that they could not express their opinions and hurts over racial issues without being labeled divisive and therefore un-Christian. This situation led to more frustration as the students of color felt they had no forum in which to make their concerns heard. The exception to this was the multicultural student programs group that was grounded in theological justifications for multiculturalism. In this group, students of color were able to find a forum to discuss racial issues from a Christian perspective. The existence of this group seems to be a major reason why many students of color are willing to stay at the college.

Other organizations we studied also actively promoted theological arguments for diversity and multiculturalism. Some drew on imagery from the book of Revelation, which describes the distinct ethnic groups coming together in the "new Jerusalem" to worship God together. Others emphasized that God created culture and therefore has gifted each one with specific and unique attributes to contribute to the church. Flowing out of these theologically driven arguments, several of the organizations made efforts to integrate culturally different styles of music, preaching, and ministry activities into the structure of the organization. Some intentionally hired leaders from diverse backgrounds in order to diversify the cultural styles represented in the organization.

Students in Christ in Action similarly drew upon theological arguments for support of racially diverse and race-specific religious groups. Some students argued that race-specific religious groups were useful for creating bridges to nonbelievers—they facilitated evangelistic efforts. Other students suggested that the Bible states that Christians should be unified, and therefore we should not have race-specific, but rather racially diverse religious organizations.

The organizations, or subgroups within those organizations, that had more explicit theological justifications for multiculturalism also were more likely to promote dialogue about racial and cultural issues. In the case of Emmanuel Bible College, the multicultural program kept students of color from leaving because of its ability to create a safe space for dialogue among students of color and its offer of a way to connect their experiences to their faith. At Wilcrest, the leadership promoted a number of opportunities to discuss racial and cultural issues that came out of their commitment to multiculturalism. These types of dialogues, while sometimes heated, seemed to stabilize the organization. They allowed for the airing of grievances and for thinking through how racial and cultural dynamics affect the organization.

At Messiah fellowship, in contrast, there was no initial promotion of a theology of multiculturalism, and no dialogue about racial and cultural issues for the first two years of the church's existence. This lack of dialogue, and lack of promotion of diversity, seems to have led to a higher level of frustration among numerical minority groups than existed in the organizations that intentionally promoted multiculturalism. When initial attempts at dialogue occurred at Messiah, there was an outpouring of frustration, followed by resistance from the majority. Since the initial discussions, however, Messiah has taken the first steps toward articulating a theology of racial reconciliation and accommodating different cultural views in the way the organization is structured. Thus, the initial dialogues produced significant structural change that seems to be ameliorating some of the frustration of the numerical minority groups.

These findings lead us to the following hypothesis:

Interracial religious organizations that actively promote theological justifications for multiculturalism are more stable than those that do not.

While the organizations that did not explicitly and actively promote a theology of multiculturalism did not necessarily promote a color-blind theology, many of their members, particularly white members, did. As a result, those members tended to squelch dialogue and criticize as divisive those who brought up racial issues. Thus, minority groups have to deal with their frustrations in silence. It appears that an organization that actively promotes a theology of multiculturalism can counteract the notion among some of its membership that talking about racial issues and embracing difference is somehow divisive. As a result these organizations seem more likely to function smoothly and to retain members, as well as to reinforce the value placed on diversity that brought many of the members to the organization in the first place.

Spiritual Enrichment as a Result of Ethnic Diversity

One of the most consistent findings in our cases was that members of these interracial organizations reported a profound sense of spiritual enrichment from worshipping God in a racially and ethnically diverse environment. Nearly all of the people we interviewed, regardless of ethnic group, saw much benefit to being in an interracial congregation. Most notably, all but a few respondents in the church cases mentioned that the diversity of the church was either a main reason for coming to the church, or one of the main things that they enjoyed about the church. Many respondents stated their appreciation for their organization's diversity in theological terms, saying that it is a more "biblical" than homogeneous church, and that it is a true representation of heaven on earth. Others stated their appreciation using more spiritual and emotional language. They felt their worship of God was more "full" or "pure" when they worshiped in an ethnically diverse setting. Some spoke of an emotional lift from singing worship songs in different languages and hearing others pray and preach in different cultural styles. Others spoke in spiritual terms of the beauty of the combination of cultures in the organization.

Interestingly, many of these comments were offered by the same people who were experiencing high levels of frustration over the way their organizations operated, or who were experiencing high levels of relational isolation. In fact, most of those we interviewed in religious organizations who were experiencing high levels of frustration and difficulty said that they would never consider going back to a homogeneous religious organization. Most of the respondents we interviewed who had left their respective organizations because of various frustrations were either attending or looking for another interracial organization. It seems that many of the members of these organizations place such a high value on worshiping in a diverse congregation that they have ruled out the option of returning to a homogeneous congregation. In addition, the spiritual benefits they receive in worshiping in a diverse setting seem to outweigh the high social costs. (Earlier in this chapter, we identified one key exception: white families with teenagers.) The sociologist Max Weber's typology of social action seems particularly relevant here. Weber argued that there are essentially four orientations that drive people to make decisions about how to order their lives.

Instrumentally rational: for the attainment of the actor's own rationally pursued and calculated ends. People driven by instrumental rationality decide what goals they want to pursue and then rationally calculate the best way to attain those goals. For example, if a person decides that the important factors in buying a house are increasing property values and high-quality schools for children, that person will research each neighborhood and calculate the best location based on those criteria.

Value rational: determined by a conscious belief in the value for its own sake of some ethical, aesthetic, religious, or other form of behavior, independently of its prospects of success. People making value rational decisions pursue courses of action they believe are right or valuable, regardless of the consequences of those actions. To continue with the example of house shopping, a person who has a religious conviction that to live among the poor is ethically or religiously valuable may buy a house in a poor neighborhood regardless of the consequences of that choice in terms of prospects for wealth, safety, or the education of their children.

Affectual: determined by the actors' specific affects and feeling states. The person driven by affectual considerations will pursue an action because of the feelings that emerge from pursuing it. The house shopper in this case may decide to purchase a particular home because it "felt right" or because they like the "atmosphere" of the neighborhood.

Traditional: determined by ingrained habituation. Finally, a person may decide to do something simply because that is the way things have always been done. A person driven by traditional considerations may purchase a home in a neighborhood because she grew up there, and her parents and grandparents lived there, and as a result she would not consider any other neighborhoods.

The decisions people make in how to order their lives often include more than one of these orientations, and people may be driven by different orientations at different times. The value of this typology is that it shows the multiple ways people order their lives, and the multiple considerations that drive people to do what they do. It also suggests distinct patterns in decision-making. Weber would argue that most, if not all, of the decisions people make are driven by at least one of these four types. It appears from our interviews that if members of these organizations were driven by instrumental rationality, most would leave these organizations. If the members were simply seeking the calculated ends of meaning, belonging, and an environment where they might experience God in a way that is consistent with their own cultural orientations, these goods are delivered much more efficiently in ethnically homogeneous religious groups (Emerson and Smith 2000). The influential "church growth movement" has recognized this fact and has promoted the idea that congregations should target specific homogeneous subcultures because it is much easier to effectively meet the needs of a homogeneous population with specific types of worship, programs, and ministry than it is to meet the needs of a heterogeneous population (Wagner 1979). What this perspective misses, and what Weber recognized, is that some people are driven by considerations other than simply "getting their needs met."

Clearly, most members of the organizations we studied experience conflicts, difficulties, and frustrations that arise from the interracial nature of these organizations. Yet they continue to be involved, and they state that they would never go back to a racially homogeneous church. While many have left these organizations and the proportions of racial and ethnic groups within them have fluctuated, they have all been able to attract new members and to retain a majority of their existing members because, it seems, of the intrinsic value placed on diversity itself and the spiritual effects of worshiping in a diverse environment.

We were surprised to find that almost all of the students of color at the evangelical college, arguably the most frustrated group in our case studies, reported that given the chance to do it all over again, they would again choose to attend EBC. They stated that despite their negative experiences, they felt that they experienced God in new ways by being at the college.

Using Weber's terminology, value and affectual rationality seem to be more influential factors than instrumental rationality in explaining the behavior of most of these members. Reports of a spiritual enrichment, a "high" feeling that "gets in your blood" when worshiping in a diverse environment seems to follow Weber's description of affectual rationality. Moreover, those who clearly articulated theological reasons for their desire to be in an interracial group seem to be operating according to Weber's description of value-rational behavior.

These descriptions explain the behavior of the members of these organizations who, despite the costs and losses incurred in being involved, continue to be committed members. For these members the act of worshiping and ministering in an interracial environment is valued for its own sake, not because it meets their needs in some way. This valuing diversity for its own sake keeps those members committed to the organization despite the fact that their instrumental goals (feeling relationally connected, finding meaning and belonging, being satisfied with the way the organization provides services) are often not attained. Moreover, for many, the subjective feeling states (the "taste of heaven") produced by the interracial environment seem to outweigh the desire to have their needs adequately met within the organization.

In sum, the spiritual and religious forces operating within these organizations produce both stabilizing and destabilizing effects. They are summarized as follows:

Destabilizing forces:
1. Religiously charged ethnocentrism
2. Color-blind theologies

Stabilizing forces:
1. Theological arguments for diversity
2. Spiritual enrichment coming from diverse worship environments

Each of the organizations we have examined contained a different mix of these forces. Interestingly, even the case study organizations that have the most destabilizing dynamics and the highest turnover still continue to draw a diverse group of new members. The ethnic mixes of our organizations have all fluctuated slightly but all, perhaps surprisingly, remain racially diverse and seem to be in no danger of collapsing. There are undoubtedly larger forces at work, perhaps divine forces, that keep these organizations going and drawing new members even in the face of these destabilizing forces.

Considering the Limits of Our Cases

As we noted at the outset of this work, to control variation and isolate racial and cultural effects, all of our case study organizations are evangelical Protestant. Do our findings generalize beyond this (albeit large) sub-group of religion? And do our findings generalize beyond religious organizations to volunteer organizations in general? We expect that many of the conclusions we reach about internal organizational dynamics and the external environment are not limited to specific cultural traditions. We believe these findings will generalize, perhaps after some tailoring, to other contexts. At the same time, for the internal spiritual dynamics, we anticipate that at least some aspects of our findings would not generalize as well, given that religious cultures can differ so dramatically. Ultimately, this chapter offers hypotheses, and they should be taken as such. The value of this work will be in people testing the hypotheses offered here in different contexts, and based on those tests, refining or restating them where needed.

Conclusion

As we discussed in the opening chapter, religious organizations occupy a unique place in U.S. civil society, serving as vital mediating organizations between the small, private worlds of individual and family and the mass public worlds of government, the economy, and public education. Here Americans come together by the millions, in hundreds of thousands of locations, day after day, week after week, year after year, to worship and construct meaning and belonging. Here the meaning of race is explicitly and implicitly created, enacted, and in some cases, rearticulated. Here social capital and social networks are developed and used to impact life far beyond the confines of these subcultures (see for example Emerson and Smith 2000: chap. 8). Here racial inequality can be addressed. Scholars have greatly underestimated the importance of such organizations for race relations and racial inequality nationally. And with the rapid rate of immigration from around the globe, what happens in religious organizations in the United States will have global impacts on the meaning of race and ethnicity.

Our findings can best be summarized using the racial formation perspective (Omi and Winant 1994; Winant 2002). *Racial formation* is the process by which racial categories are created, inhabited, altered, or destroyed. This process takes place through social interaction and over time. It occurs by linking representations of what race is and what it means to structures (practices, organizations). This linking is achieved via racial projects. *Racial projects* seek to define and interpret racial dynamics and distribute resources along racial lines. According to racial formation theory, society is infused with racial projects. Everyone learns some combination of these projects, shaping their understanding of race.

So what does this mean for our case studies, and for race relations more broadly? The groups we studied are volunteer organizations. As we noted in the opening chapter, they provide us with perhaps the clearest possible view of what people do when allowed to choose. At the institutional level, people clearly tend to choose to affiliate with people who are racially like themselves. This is in part due to cultural and social network differences, but as we saw in our case studies, it is also in part due to maintaining racial difference (see also DeYoung et al. 2003: chaps. 6 and 7). The organizations we studied are also religious. People expect more of others and have higher standards in such situations. In short, the stakes are raised.

We focused on those cases where people were in interracial religious organizations. In these intimate settings, what racial projects occurred, and what can we conclude about racial formation? Clearly within each organization we found competing racial projects. Typically we witnessed struggles as the racial projects of different groups competed for influence. Would this be an organization in which unity is stressed in a way that excluded diversity? Would it be an organization that worships in the style of one racial group, or will it attempt to worship in multiple styles? Who will be in leadership and does it matter? Would numerical majority group members form dense same-race friendship networks, leaving others isolated? The negotiation of these different racial projects by overlapping groups within the organizations constitutes the process of racial formation. This process continually shapes members' views of race as well as relations between members of different racial groups.

In some cases, the racial projects that win the day and are institutionalized are harmful to race relations; they reproduce structures of superiority/inferiority based on race categories. Included here are color-blind racial projects that seek to practice only "Christianity" or "Bible-based faith" without examining how race and culture affect interpretations and expressions of this faith. In each racial project of this type in our case studies, we found this meant favoring one cultural interpretation of the good and right over others. In such interracial organizations, the fears of those who oppose such organizations are realized.

But we also found cases that challenged racial inequality and improved race relations, at least for the members involved in the organization (and because their members live good portions of their lives elsewhere, perhaps beyond the organization). These racial projects usually gained influence as the percentage of the nondominant groups in the organization increased, as well as over time and through negotiation and rearticulation of key symbols within the faith (see Becker 1999 for an extended example of rearticulation). At the individual level, this might mean the loss of members of the numerical majority group, especially if that group is white, but other numerical majority group members often replaced them.

Interracial religious organizations face many obstacles, many destabilizing forces. Being part of a larger racialized society, interracial religious organizations can go the way of the larger society, institutionalizing inequality. In short, interracial religious organizations can be places that simply recreate racial division, as critics of such organizations charge.

But we have seen that this is too simple a view. Members of these organizations, at least in the United States, typically chose to be members. As detailed in Emerson and Smith (2000: chaps. 7 and 8), this volunteer aspect of religious organizations gives tremendous power to the members themselves. As such, numerical minority members and groups can often eventually influence the racial formation process of the congregation. If they do not, they typically will leave to try somewhere else.

We see through our research that the reproduction of racial inequality appears often to be true in the early stages of interracial organizations, but these organizations are difficult to maintain indefinitely with such one-sided arrangements. People can and do leave when they feel excluded. While an individual may stay in a bad marriage, a whole racial group will rarely stay in a bad volunteer organization. They have too many other choices. And the costs of leaving are less (they do not lose their income or a developed circle of friends by leaving). If they are going to stay, then they will continue to negotiate for change. Leaders, if they value being interracial, must adjust their racial understandings and practices. Thus in the final analysis, interracial organizations, if they are to survive, cannot reproduce racial inequality to the same degree as the larger society. Members eventually leave under such circumstances. This means that given time to develop, interracial volunteer organizations will, against all odds, break down racial inequality. They will do so for both current and future generations.

But social life, of course, is never so clear-cut. Important exceptions to the hopeful picture presented above often arise. Sometimes numerical minority groups, perhaps because of the particular mix of people, are completely co-opted by the numerical majority group such that they come to adopt the racial projects of the majority group.[5] Sometimes this co-option occurs because numerical minority group members are so dedicated to the value of interracial organizations that they tolerate and even accept unhealthy organizations. Sometimes numerical minority groups do not grow large enough to challenge the status quo. According to past research, a minimum 20 percent non-majority is needed to affect the numerical majority group. Our case studies revealed another exception. We might call it the micro/macro disjuncture. At the individual level, numerical minority group members may leave an organization that is not responsive to them, but if they are continually replaced by new numerical minority group members willing to tolerate inequality for a time, the numerical minority group may never have an impact commensurate with its numbers. In this way, the structure can stay the same precisely because the people do not.

Interracial religious organizations provide a visible stage on which to observe interracial projects and human relations develop. Due to both their volunteer and religious nature, the pressures they encounter on this stage are immense. The drama that unfolds as humans attempt to articulate and practice their highest ideals demands attention. This stage, situated between the private and public worlds of contemporary life, has much to teach the larger society. Both the failures and successes of these organizations show in bold relief how dynamic, racial-inequality-challenging organizations can be fashioned and lived out.

Notes

NOTE TO CHAPTER 1

1. We define "evangelical" as those people, groups, and organizations who believe that the Bible is the final and ultimate authority, that salvation is only achieved by placing one's faith in Jesus Christ, that this "good news" should be shared with others, and that this faith should be taken beyond the evangelical subculture to engage the larger society and culture.

NOTES TO CHAPTER 4

1. This account of the theological positions of the church during the split is based solely upon interviews with current longtime members who were a part of the "grace" camp. Hence, the depiction may be biased against those who left the church. However, whatever the specifics of the reasons for this division, we can safely say that this split was theologically rather than racially based.

2. Demographic data provided on Mapleton and Anderson is from the 2000 census.

3. Overall, whites reported less frustration with Crosstown than did African Americans, and two white respondents reported having no frustrations with the church.

4. The gender and number of children of respondents may have been changed to further conceal their identities.

5. This is based upon data the youth pastor collected on the youth group in 2000.

NOTE TO CHAPTER 5

1. We only interviewed members who attended the 11 o'clock service.

NOTE TO CHAPTER 6

1. Gaertner et al. (1989, 1999) argue that diverse organizations can become more cohesive if they allow space for subordinate groups to maintain their separate subordinate identities.

NOTES TO CHAPTER 8

1. Most of the racial transitioning occurred during the 1970s.

2. This phenomenon has also been noted in other cases. See Foster (1997) and Foster and Brelsford (1996).

3. Emerson et al. (2001) similarly found that the racial composition of neighborhoods matters particularly for white families with children under eighteen years old. Among white households, these families are least likely to live in neighborhoods with African Americans.

4. Saporito and Lareau (1999) also found that white families are averse to choosing schools for their children that are predominantly African-American.

5. For simplicity's sake, we talk here as if groups form perfectly along racial lines, where racial projects and interests also align perfectly along racial lines. In practice, there are always a few bridge people who occupy space between these groups, and a few people who align with a racially other group.

References

Ammerman, Nancy T. 1997. *Congregation and Community*. New Brunswick, N.J.: Rutgers University Press.

Anderson, Deborah, and David Shapiro. 1996. "Racial Differences in Access to High-Paying Jobs and the Wage Gap Between Black and White Women." *Industrial and Labor Relations Review* 49:273–286.

Beaman, Lori G. 2003. "The Myth of Pluralism, Diversity, and Vigor: The Constitutional Privilege of Protestantism in the United States and Canada." *Journal for the Scientific Study of Religion* 42:311–325.

Becker, Penny Edgell. 1999. *Congregations in Conflict: Cultural Models of Local Religious Life*. New York: Cambridge University Press.

Bonilla-Silva, Eduardo. 2001. *White Supremacy and Racism in the Post–Civil Rights Era*. Boulder, Colo.: Lynne Reiner Publishers.

Carroll, Glenn R. 1984. "Organizational Ecology." *Annual Review of Sociology* 10:71–93.

Cnaan, Ram A. 2002. *The Invisible Caring Hand: American Congregations and the Provision of Welfare*. New York: New York University Press.

Collins, Sharon M. 1995. *Black Corporate Executives: The Making and Breaking of Black Middle Class*. Philadelphia, Pa.: Temple University Press.

DeYoung, Curtiss P., Michael O. Emerson, George Yancey, and Karen Chai Kim. 2003. *United by Faith: The Multiracial Congregation as an Answer to the Problem of Race*. New York: Oxford University Press.

Doane, Ashley W. 2003. "Rethinking Whiteness Studies." In *White Out: The Continuing Significance of Racism*, edited by Ashley W. Doane and Eduardo Bonilla-Silva. New York: Routledge.

Dougherty, Kevin D. 2003. "How Monochromatic Is Church Membership? Racial-Ethnic Diversity in Religious Community." *Sociology of Religion* 64: 65–85.

Durkeim, Emile. 1912. *The Elementary Forms of Religious Life*. New York: The Free Press.

Ebaugh, Helen Rose, and Janet Saltzman Chavez. 2000. *Religion and the New Immigrants: Continuities and Adaptations in Immigrant Congregations*. Walnut Creek, Calif.: Altamira Press.

Eck, Dianna L. 2001. *A New Religious America: How a "Christian Country" Has Now Become the World's Most Religiously Diverse Nation*. San Francisco: HarperSanFrancisco.

Emerson, Michael O. Forthcoming. *People of the Dream*.

Emerson, Michael O., and Karen Chai Kim. 2003. "Multiracial Congregations: A Typology and Analysis of Their Development." *Journal for the Scientific Study of Religion* 42:217–227.

Emerson, Michael O., and Christian Smith. 2000. *Divided by Faith: Evangelical Religion and the Problem of Race in America*. New York: Oxford University Press.

Emerson, Michael O., George Yancey, and Karen J. Chai. 2001. "Does Race Matter in Residential Segregation? Exploring the Preferences of White Americans." *American Sociological Review* 66:922–935

Feagin, Joe R., Hernán Vera, and Pinar Batur. 2001. *White Racism: The Basics*. Second Edition. New York: Routledge.

Finke, Roger, and Rodney Stark. 1992. *The Churching of America, 1776–1990: Winners and Losers in Our Religious Economy*. New Brunswick, N.J.: Rutgers University Press.

Flory, R. W. 1997. *Development and Transformation within Protestant Fundamentalism: Fundamentalist Bible Institutes and Colleges in the U.S. 1925–1991*. Unpublished doctoral dissertation, University of Chicago.

Foster, Charles R. 1997. *Leadership in Multicultural Congregations: Embracing Diversity*. Bethesda, Md.: The Alban Institute, Inc.

Foster, Charles R., and Theodore Brelsford. 1996. *We Are the Church Together: Cultural Diversity in Congregational Life*. Valley Forge, Pa.: Trinity Press.

Fosu, A. K. 1993. "Do Black and White Women Hold Different Jobs in the Same Occupation? A Critical Analysis of the Clerical and Service Sectors." *The Review of the Black Political Economy* (spring): 67–81.

Frankenberg, Ruth. 1993. *White Women, Race Matters: The Social Construction of Whiteness*. Minneapolis: University of Minnesota Press.

Frazier, E. Franklin. 1974. *The Negro Church in America*. New York: Schocken Books.

Frey, William H. 1985. "Mover Destination Selectivity and the Changing Suburbanization of Metropolitan Whites and Blacks." *Demography* 22:223–243.

Frey, William H., and Reynolds Farley. 1996. "Latino, Asian, and Black Segregation in U.S. Metropolitan Areas: Are Multi-ethnic Metros Different?" *Demography* 33:35–50.

Gaertner, Samuel L., John F. Dovidio, Jason A. Nier, Christine M. Ward, and Brenda S. Banker. 1999. "Across Cultural Divides: The Values of a Superordinate Identity." In *Cultural Divides: Understanding and Overcoming Group Conflict*, edited by Deborah A. Prentice and Dale T. Miller. New York: Russell Sage Foundation.

Gaertner, Samuel L., Jeffrey Mann, Audrey Murrell, and John F. Dovidio. 1989. "Reducing Intergroup Bias: The Benefits of Recategorization." *Journal of Personality and Social Psychology* 57:239–249.

Goodwin, Carole. 1979. *The [Mapleton] Strategy: Community Control of Racial Change.* Chicago: University of Chicago Press.

Hadaway, C. Kirk. 1981. "The Demographic Environment on Church Membership Change." *Journal for the Scientific Study of Religion* 20: 77–89.

Hannan, M. T., and J. Freeman. 1977. "The Population Ecology of Organizations." *American Journal of Sociology* 82:929–964.

Hurtado, S., J. F. Milem, A. R. Clayton-Pederson, and W. R. Allen. 1999. *Enacting Diverse Learning Environments: Improving the Climate for Racial/Ethnic Diversity in Higher Education.* Washington, D.C.: George Washington University Press.

Jackson, Kenneth T. 1985. *Crabgrass Frontier: The Suburbanization of the United States.* New York: Oxford University Press.

Johnson, Heather Beth, and Thomas M. Shapiro. 2003. "Good Neighbors, Good Schools: Race and the 'Good Choices' of White Families." In *White Out: The Continuing Significance of Racism,* edited by Ashley W. Doane and Eduardo Bonilla-Silva. New York: Routledge.

Lincoln, C. Eric, and Lawrence H. Mamiya. 1990. *The Black Church in the African American Experience.* Durham, N.C.: Duke University Press.

Lipsitz, George. 1998. *The Possessive Investment in Whiteness: How White People Profit from Identity Politics.* Philadelphia, Pa.: Temple University Press.

Massey, Douglas S., and Nancy Denton. 1993. *American Apartheid.* Cambridge: Harvard University Press.

Mays, Benjamin, and Joseph W. Nicholson. 1985. "The Genius of the Negro Church." In *Afro-American Religious History: A Documentary Witness,* edited by Milton C. Sernett, 337–348. Durham, N.C.: Duke University Press.

McKenzie, Evan. 2000. *The Politics of School Desegregation in [Mapleton]. A Great Cities Institute Working Paper.* University of Illinois at Chicago.

McPherson, J. M., P. A. Popielarz, and S. Drobnic. 1992. "Social Networks and Organizational Dynamics." *American Sociological Review* 57: 153–170.

Morris, Aldon D. 1984. *The Origins of the Civil Rights Movement: Black Communities Organizing for Change.* New York: The Free Press.

Musil, C. 1999. *To Form a More Perfect Union: Campus Diversity Issues.* Washington, D.C.: Association of American Colleges and Universities.

Naylor, L. L. 1999. "Introduction to American Cultural Diversity: Unresolved Questions, Issues, and Problems." In *Problems and Issues of Diversity in the United States,* ed. L. L. Naylor (Westport, Conn.: Bergin & Garvey).

Olson, Daniel V. A. 1993. "Fellowship Ties and the Transmission of Religious Identity." In *Beyond Establishment,* edited by Jackson Carroll and Wade Clark Roof, 32–53. Louisville, Ky.: Westminster/John Knox Press.

Omi, Michael, and Howard Winant. 1994. *Racial Formation in the United States: From the 1960s to the 1990s.* New York: Routledge.

Popielarz, P. A., and J. M. McPherson. 1995. "On the Edge or In Between: Niche Position, Niche Overlap, and the Duration of Voluntary Association Memberships." American Journal of Sociology 101: 698–721.

Putnam, Robert D. 2000. *Bowling Alone: The Collapse and Revival of American Community.* New York: Simon & Schuster.

Rossi, P. H. 1980. *Why Families Move.* Beverly Hills, Calif.: Sage Publications.

Saporito, Salvatore, and Annette Lareau. 1999. "School Selection as a Process: The Multiple Dimensions of Race in Framing Educational Choice." *Social Problems* 46: 418–440.

Singh, J. V., and C. J. Lumsden. 1990. "Theory and Research in Organizational Ecology." *Annual Review of Sociology* 16:161–195.

Tatum, Beverly Daniel. 1997. *Why Are All the Black Kids Sitting Together in the Cafeteria?* New York: Basic Books.

Tomaskovic-Devey, Donald. 1993. *Gender and Racial Inequality at Work: The Sources and Consequences of Job Segregation.* Ithaca, N.Y.: ILR Press.

Tucker, C. Jack, and William L. Urton. 1987. "Frequency of Geographic Mobility: Findings from the National Health Interview Survey." *Demography* 24:265–270.

U. S. Congregational Life Survey. 2000. Cynthia Woolever, principal investigator. Louisville, Ky.: Presbyterian Church (USA).

Wagner, C. P. 1979. *Our Kind of People: The Ethical Dimensions of Church Growth in America.* Atlanta, Ga.: John Knox Press.

Wedam, E. 1999. "Ethno-Racial Diversity within Indianapolis Congregations." *Research Notes* 2, no. 4.

Wellman, David T. 1977. *Portraits of White Racism.* New York: Cambridge University Press.

Wilson, Frank Harold. 1995. "Rising Tide or Ebb Tide? Recent Changes in the Black Middle Class in the U.S., 1980–1990." *Research in Race and Ethnic Relations* 8:21–55.

Winant, Howard. 2002. *The World Is a Ghetto: Race and Democracy since World War II.* New York: Basic Books.

Wuthnow, Robert, and John H. Evans, eds. 2002. *The Quiet Hand of God: Faith Based Activism and the Public Role of Mainline Protestantism.* Berkeley: University of California Press.

Index

Acceptance, feeling of, 85–87, 90
Adaptation, 3
African Americans: worship and preaching styles, 24–26; friendship networks of, 64, 115–117
Anderson, 62; businesses in, 62; racial compositions of, 62; socioeconomic composition of, 62
Animists(s), 38
Apartment(s), 49
Assimilation, 2, 3

Baptist(s), 36, 38
Belonging, 14–24, 33, 151–161
Benefits, of diversity, 13–14, 32–33, 35, 89–90, 157, 178–181
Black Pentecostal churches, 42
Brookside, 7, 80–103, 124
Buddhists, 38
Bulletin, 38
Budget, 36, 54

Case studies, 4, 5
Case summary (Table 1.1), 7
Catholic(s), 6, 38
Church culture (of Crosstown), 63, 78; friendliness and warmth, 63, 78
Choices, 4
Christ in Action, 7, 104–108, 111–115; Asian attenders of,
111–115; member participation of, 107–108; racial composition of, 106; and Reach, 107
Civil society, 3
Cliques, 15–24, 52, 112–113
Color-blind ideal, 139–141, 149, 175–176
Community service, 85
Congregations, 3
Contact theory, 156
Core members, 55
Costs, of diversity, 157, 159
Crosstown Community Church, 7, 58–79; history of, 50–60; racial composition of, 60; and racial transition, 58; religious affiliation of, 58, 59, 60; socioeconomic composition of, 60
Cultural differences, 159–160, 174

Decreasing stack method, 5
Desegregation, 2, 3
Dialogues, about racial issues, 29–31, 176–177
Diversity, 4, 6, 13–14, 32–33, 35, 38, 41, 50, 51–56, 59, 65–68, 89–90, 117–118, 145–147, 157, 178–181; African American views on, 66, 118; Asian views on, 117, 118; white views on, 66–67, 118

Division, in Crosstown Community Church, 59–60
Durkheim, Emile, 174
Dutch immigrants, 81–82

Emmanuel Bible College, 7, 126–150
Equipment, 54
Evangelical(s): and Crosstown Community Church, 59; colleges, 127; subculture of, 138–143
Evangelism, 109, 110
Ethnocentrism, religion and, 33–35, 148, 173–175
Exclusion/excluded, 14–24, 43, 87–89, 133–135, 151–161
Exit interviews, 48
External socioeconomic structures, 161–173

Filipino churches, 10–11
Filipinos, 10; expressing conflict, 22; social relationships, 15–24; time and, 26–28
"First-timers," 38
Foreign-born. *See* Immigration/immigrants
Friendship networks, 1, 14–24, 43, 45–48, 52, 64–66, 87–89, 109–114, 116–117, 123–125, 133–135, 151–161; of African Americans, 64, 115–117; of Asians, 112–113, 123; of Christ in Action attenders, 110–112, 114; of Crosstown attenders, 64–65; interracial, 66, 76, 78; of Reach attenders, 116–117; same-race, 64, 125; of whites, 64
Fundamentalism, Bible colleges and, 128

Germany, 42
Group size, 48

Hispanics, language issues, 91–93
Home, feeling of, 85–87
Homogeneous churches and religious groups, 4, 13–14
Houston, 7, 36, 40, 49, 50

Immigration/immigrants, 3, 37, 38, 39, 41, 44, 46, 52, 55–57, 132
Individualism, 131, 136, 140–141, 148
Integration, 2, 3, 4
Interracial, 58, 66–67, 76, 78; families, 11–12, 42, 45, 66–67, 78, 154, 165–166; friendships, 76, 78
Isolation, social, 14–24, 43, 133–135, 149

Koreans, 129–130

Language, 91–93
Leaders, of Crosstown Community Church, 58, 60
Leaving (neighborhoods).*See*Move/ing (fromandtoneighborhoods)
Los Angeles, racial composition, 10, 81–82
Love, atmosphere of, 85–87, 90, 102

Majority group, 33, 59, 64, 79, 149, 154, 156; African Americans as, 59, 64
Mapleton, 61–62; businesses in, 61; and community activists, 62; racial composition of, 61–62; and racial diversity programs, 61; socioeconomic composition of, 61
Marriages, interracial, 11–12, 42, 45, 66–67,78, 154, 165–166
Messiah Fellowship, 7, 8, 9–35, 36, 39, 45, 52, 56, 64–65, 77, 79
Minority group, 59, 64, 79; at Messiah, 64; social isolation of, 33,

149, 156; turnover of, 154; whites as, 59, 79
Mission statements, 61, 105, 109; of Christ in Action, 105, 109; of Crosstown, 61
Mobility, 155–156
Move/ing (fromandtoneighborhoods), 48, 49–51, 55
Multiculturalism, 143–144, 176–178
Music. *See* Worship

Neighborhood, 37, 42, 49, 50, 58–59, 61, 68, 76; composition, 162–165; racial transition, 58–76; white flight, 61, 68
Networks, 3
Niche edge effect, 153
Niche overlap effect, 153
Numerical minorities: social isolation of, 33, 149, 156; turnover of, 154

Offensive remarks, 132
Oil bust, in Houston, 36
Oppression, 52
Organization, structure of, 28–29, 31–32, 159–160
Organizational dynamics, 151–161
Outside members. *See* Peripheral members

Pentecostal(s), 129
Peripheral members, 55
Physical plant, 36
Pluralism, 2, 3
Population ecology, 166
Postmodernism, 143–144
Power, 38
Preaching, cultural styles, 24–26, 98–99
Prejudice, 49, 50, 158
Pre-millennialism, 131
Protestant(s), 6

Punctuality, 1, 26–28, 32, 33, 173
Race-specific groups, 105, 106, 118–123; Reach, 106; attenders' views on, 118–122
Racial: justice, 144, 149; formation, 182, 185
Racial transition, 58, 68, 77, 78
Racism, 52, 170
Reconciliation, racial, 31–32, 144

Sagemont, 36
Secular academia, 130–131
Segregation, 3, 4; in denominations, 128–129
Separation, 2
Small groups, 22–24
Social: isolation, 14–24; ties, 64, 110, 111
Socioeconomic status, 45
South Urban University, 104–106
Southern Baptist. *See* Baptist(s)
Southern California, 7
Spanish, 40, 44, 48, 54, 57; worship in, 84; incorporation of, 91–93
Spiritual benefits of diversity, 13–14, 32–33, 35, 89–90, 157, 178–181
Structure, organizational, 28–29, 31–32, 159–161
Subgroups, within organizations, 157–158
Survey, 39
"Switchers," 38
Symbols, 60

Theological: arguments for color-blindness, 175–176; arguments for multiculturalism, 176–178; significance of diversity, 13–14, 32
Time, church services and, 26–28, 32, 33, 53, 173
Turnover, 45

Vision statement, 31, 37, 42, 55
Volunteer organizations, 3, 183

Weber, Max, 179–180
White flight, 162–163; African American views on, 67–70, 76, 79; blacks' experiences with, 76, 79; white views on, 70–72
White flux, 78
Whites, 58, 59, 72–76, 112; commitment of, 84–85; concerns about youth programs, 71–72, 168–171; dominance in society, 167–173; evangelical subculture of, 138, 176; expectations of, 101; expressing conflict, 22; feeling rejection from, 94–97; leaving organizations, 100–101, 167–173; in the

minority, 34, 59; social interaction among, 102–103; time and, 26–28; views on Asian "cliques," 112; who left Crosstown, 58, 72–76
Wilcrest, 7, 36–57, 58, 63, 64–65, 77, 79, 124
Woo, Pastor Rodney, 37–38, 40–41, 44, 49, 50–51, 57
Woo, Sasha, 57
Worship, music styles, 24–25, 34, 42, 53–54, 56, 84, 100, 174

Youth pastors, 72, 75, 77
Youth programs, 71–72, 74, 75, 76, 77, 168–171; black parents' views on, 75; and teen interracial friendship, 74; white parents' views on, 71–72

About the Authors

BRAD CHRISTERSON is Associate Professor of Sociology at Biola University. He has written extensively on ethnicity and its effects on organizations and global capitalism.

KORIE EDWARDS is Assistant Professor of Sociology at The Ohio State University. Her research interests include race and ethnicity, sociology of religion, and social stratification.

MICHAEL O. EMERSON is Professor of Sociology at the University of Notre Dame, director of the Du Bois Center for the Advanced Study of Religion and Race, and author, with Christian Smith, of *Divided by Faith: Evangelical Religion and the Problem of Race in America*, which received the 2001 Distinguished Book Award from the Society for the Scientific Study of Religion.